Decoding d-Commerce

Decoding d-Commerce

10+ Years of CPG Experiments in Byte Sized Chunks

Marc Warburton

CONTENTS

CHAPTER 5. D-COMMERCE DECODED

CHAPTER 6. BILL GATES WAS WRONG

CONCLUSION. TEN GIGA-BYTES

AFTERWORD TO THE SECOND EDITION

WORDS OF THANKS

ABOUT THE AUTHOR

Marc Warburton has worked in CPG for over twenty years and is an established thought leader in Digital Commerce. He has worked across a broad range of business types, categories and markets, providing strategic advice, leadership and guidance regarding the impact of the Digital Revolution on our working lives. Marc is passionate about helping brands quickly decomplexify the digital world and see everything through the shopper's eyes. He has contributed to a range of conferences, media articles and forums all relating to the  goal of making Shopper Marketing and Digital Commerce more valuable disciplines in CPG. He lives in Cheltenham with his wife, three children and Cockapoos.

FOREWORD TO THE SECOND EDITION

'Once you start working in digital you'll never want to do anything else'.

WHEN I STARTED working 'in digital' over ten years ago, I honestly did not have a clue what to do. What I was actually trying to do, was to manage my career with a move back into Marketing: an opportunity came up to report into the Marketing Director with responsibility for e-Commerce and Digital Marketing, that sounded like fun, and I have not really looked back since.

Fast forward over ten years, and our wonderful world of Consumer Packaged Goods (CPG) has in some ways changed beyond recognition, although in other ways it is very much still the same. We are still devoting our best efforts to surprising and delighting our consumers and shoppers; maybe now we just need a different toolkit to do this to the best of our abilities.

Most valuable brand in the world ten years ago? Coca-Cola. Coca-Cola's position in the rankings in 2021? Just outside the top 5 and out-fizzed, hardly surprisingly, by a load of tech players (Apple, Google, Microsoft,

Amazon and Facebook in that order[1]). Tech players that were there, but not really there, only such a short space of time ago. What did we do before Google anyhow?

The whole idea of 'Brand Value' has changed at a fundamental level: traditional notions of brand marketing have been pilloried by Byron Sharp[2], and the shift in the balance of power between brand and shopper is paramount. Marketers used to defend a one percent increase in volume on deal with religious fanaticism; the only thing that keeps the marketer at the helm of some CPG businesses today is legacy's power to endure.

The retailers too are evolving. New partnerships and strategies are paying dividends for some; others sadly fall by the wayside as their pace of change fails to match that of the world around them. This is being driven, for the most part, by the emergence of the digitally enabled shopper.

The purpose of this book is to impart some tips and tricks picked up over the last ten plus years spent navigating this wonderful melting pot of opportunity. There have definitely been some mistakes made along the way (some clangers as you will see); but I dare to think I may have uncovered some rough diamonds too.

Indeed, this whole 'experimentation' mentality is absolutely fundamental to succeeding in today's Digital Commerce environment. Keep your eyes wide open with a keen willingness to learn and self-improve. Do this and you will both be in good company and significantly improve your chances of commercial success.

The following six chapters are loosely structured around the different parts of my digital career: setting up e-Commerce and Digital Marketing at United Biscuits (UB); heading up eBusiness at Danone; leading Digital and Trade Marketing at Pukka Herbs; being a freelance Digital

---

[1] Forbes. "The World's Most Valuable Brands 2021"; https://www.forbes.com/powerful-brands/list/ (accessed March 07, 2022).
[2] Byron Sharp, *How brands grow. What marketers don't know*, (Sydney, Oxford University Press, 2010).

Consultant in businesses such as Coca-Cola; founding my own Digital Commerce consultancy. The final chapter is a new addition for the second edition, and covers what has evolved in the world of online shopping and Daedal in the period 2020 to 2022 – so quite a lot!

The inclusions in each chapter are more or less congruent with those particular episodes; only one or two have been moved around to help with the overall storytelling. Each chapter ends with a section on data, because love it or loathe it (and I have done both), we need to keep it front of mind. I have dropped a 'byte sized' summary at the end of each chapter as well.

I have opted for the term 'Digital Commerce' (d-Commerce) as I believe that is the best catch all for what this book is about: understanding how CPG shoppers are influenced by digital means to purchase a product.

I believe 'e-Commerce' can be too narrow: it only talks of 'Purchase Journeys' completed on websites in my view. However it should be noted that e-Commerce and d-Commerce are now fairly interchangeable, with some brands opting for one and others the other.

d-Commerce does not include transactions completed solely via Electronic Data Interchange (EDI). It does include all those transactions where there is an opportunity to influence the shopper's purchase decision process via digital means.

This purchase decision process could be completed in grocery Bricks & Clicks (Dotcoms), Pure Play, Business to Business (B2B), Direct to Consumer (D2C), Marketplaces or in the newest subchannel of all: Quick Commerce (also sometimes referred to as Rapid Grocery Delivery). It could also include Purchase Journeys that dip in and out of online channels. By this definition, winning at d-Commerce therefore also includes developing a solid understanding of Omnichannel Shopper Marketing.

My final introductory undertone is one on the spirit of collaboration, or just the value of sharing learning as it could also be called. I was fortunate enough to be steered in the right direction when I started out by a chap who is now very senior at Unilever. As a homage to him I have entitled this foreword with something he said to me during our first meeting, and by Jove was he right.

This instilled in me a genuine desire to also help others along the d-Commerce path, hence my creation of what did not exist when I started out: a practical CPG d-Commerce guide.

d-Commerce in the sense defined in this book is *the* future of CPG. This is the simple and single reason why it is essential that you think about it, plan for it, and take corresponding action regarding it, in your business right now.

So I really hope you enjoy and benefit from this little book.

CHAPTER 1. CREATING THE BASICS

No smartphone, no Facebook account. Let's go for it.

THERE IS ONLY a handful of ubiquitous catch phrases in d-Commerce today, and one of these is 'Fix the Basics'. This really is good advice: sort out your images, sort out your nomenclature, sort out your search strategy and you will be off to a good start. Fix the basics, then maintain the basics, then move on.

There are plenty of examples of best practice basics accessible via LinkedIn if you want a quick point of reference here. Most businesses now have Fixing the Basics on their radar or even in their electronic out tray; more on what this means and how to do it to follow.

It is a positive thing that the industry has lined up behind the Fix the Basics rallying cry. I think this also elucidates two other related points: the lack of wider established best practice in d-Commerce, and the need to give clear guidance on what the d-Commerce basics are in the first place. I will deal with the latter of these two points first.

The world of CPG is a very busy place. There is plenty of work to do, plenty of work created, and in most businesses an opportunity to improve prioritisation to boot. The advent of 'digital' has scaled up this opportunity exponentially: there is just so much stuff out there that no one can physically be the master of every piece of digital knowledge, or even the bearer of it. Consequently, it is nonsensical to try to be.

However, we would do well to be distracted by the valuable pursuits that lie within all this digital noise. But how can we know which pursuits constitute valuable distractions and which are a bit of a waste of time? Put another way, how can we know which distractions will be good for our business health and deliver commercial gain, and which may be injurious to it, only sapping valuable resources?

These 'Unhealthy Distractions' may be quite technical: social commerce; headless commerce; for most businesses sophisticated data management technology {*insert the latest iteration of DMP, DSP, CDP in here*} to name a few. The Unhealthy Distractions may also be more structural. After all, in the kingdom of the blind, the one-eyed man is king.

Beware the CEO Pet Project or single piece of 'killer insight' that has the potential to erroneously inform an entire business digital mentality. We need to be able to filter out all these Unhealthy Distractions and focus our attentions instead on the 'Healthy Distractions'.

Healthy Distractions are the areas where there would be a benefit to spending our business's time. For example, these may include creating a Perfect Online Store, collaborating on execution projects, understanding our retailers and shoppers and so forth. All of these are much more healthy places for a business to be focusing its digital efforts.

The way to filter the Unhealthy Distractions from the Healthy ones is to create the filtering framework that your business uses. This will enable you to credibly point your business in the direction of 'what to do', whilst steering it away from 'what not to do'. This can be seen as instilling a wider 'Basics Focus' from which many businesses may benefit.

This also plays to the wider point on lack of industry best practice, and the potential impact this may have on your nascent digital team. Most digital folk have been in the position where they are the go to fixer for all business matters that require a digital point of view. These might be 'simple' things such as an investment question, 'unfair' things such as comprehensive understanding of a retailer's search algorithm, or even 'let's just lob the digital hospital pass in that direction' things such as an expectancy for in depth knowledge of all hardware operation.

Without established best practice, how can our digital folk hope to proffer a sensible response to these kinds of questions that the business feels comfortable with?

I think we should see this lack of widely accepted best practice as an opportunity: we are actually in the golden days of d-Commerce industry evolution. We can choose to see this lack of best practice as a blessing or a curse.

Some may see this as a curse for the reason described above: potential for little clarity on what to do. The lack of best practice and oversight may also mean that the digital team is largely left to its own devices. However, I think we should see this absence of legacy as a blessing: it is something that can be very liberating if properly managed.

As I shall argue throughout this book, to win in d-Commerce we need to foster a true spirit of experimentation. One where we need to be on the front foot and jump on the real opportunities quickly. One where our retail partners come to us first for advice and support.

Providing that your digital team keeps up its end of the bargain and delivers a credible digital plan, I would encourage you to enable its freedom of operation in your business as far as practical. This way you can turn this best practice vacuum into an opportunity for your business to shine.

The way to bring together this Basics Focus and lack of established best practice is through deployment of the right digital framework. One which nicely strikes the balance of focusing efforts in the right direction whilst also giving the right amount of breathing space.

Creating this kind of framework was essential when I started my first digital role, especially as I had no smartphone, no Facebook account, and no idea as already explained. I needed both a credible, insight-based plan, and a ready-made filtering device for the slew of potential digital distractions.

Which brings us nicely on to:

The 4 Ps of online success.

'The 4 P Framework' has been the mainstay of my decoding d-Commerce journey over the last ten years. For the keen eyed amongst you, you may also have clocked the subtle reference to this provided via the illustration on the front cover.

As we shall see, 'The Framework' has been deployed on a number of occasions with slightly different iterations each time. However, what has been common throughout is the effect of The Framework on providing a clear and credible view of where to focus a business's digital efforts. 'The 4 Ps' cover all elements you would expect to find in Fix the Basics, plus one or two other bits as well.

I have always been a big fan of the four-box model advocated by Stephen Covey[3] and others, which helps us understand the most effective way to spend our time. This model also serves well as a proxy for the essence of The 4 P approach.

---

[3] Stephen R Covey, *The 7 Habits of Highly Effective People*, (London, Simon & Schuster UK, 1999).

Figure 1: Model of how time can be spent in businesses.

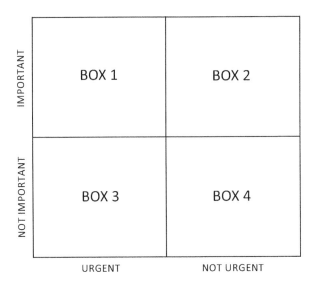

To explain this Boston Matrix briefly, consider how it is possible to split the way people spend their time in businesses along two different axes: high and low urgency, and high and low importance.

What this means, is that in business we can spend time focusing on one of four things: things that are Urgent and Important (Box 1), things that are Not Urgent and Important (Box 2), things that are Urgent and Not Important (Box 3), and things that are Not Urgent and Not Important (Box 4).

The daily culture of CPG business is typically one of urgency, with perennial time also devoted (in an urgent way of course) to the nominally non-urgent tasks such as annual planning; so far so good. Using the model above, we can also think about all those tasks as either important or non-important ones as well.

Again, most of CPG time is spent in the Urgent and Important Box 1: customer meetings or requests; copy deadlines; consumer complaints; that sort of thing. This is completely fair enough and needed to keep the wheels turning. But where is the next biggest chunk of time spent?

I cannot speak for all businesses, but in the ones where I have worked there is a fair amount of time spent in the Urgent and Not Important Box 3: the process for processes sake; the pointless meetings; the molehill mountains etc. Of course, the tasks completed in this box are not really urgent in any value adding sense at all. There is no business benefit from spending time in Box 3.

This box can be a comfort blanket and a hiding place for some; it is a hindrance and lifeblood sapper for your business. However, because tasks in this box are 'urgent', they can be accepted as necessary and not meaningfully questioned.

(And let us discount outright any debate on the value of spending time in the Not Urgent and Not Important Box 4).

What Covey points out, and I completely agree with, is that we need to spend more time in the Not Urgent and Important Box 2. This is where the magic happens, where lasting change can be invoked and consequently endures.

But how do you work out what the Box 2 foci should be for d-Commerce? Of equal importance, how do you convince a big multinational that you have identified the right Box 2 things to do at all?

What I did, was deploy a technique I was taught by a mentor a few years earlier. In brief, I applied to Dragons' Den on the back of an idea, and the BBC explained that to progress I needed a Business Plan. Fortunately, I knew someone who knew someone, who also knew someone (funnily enough they were all called Paul) who invested in start-up businesses.

In true philanthropic Gates-esque style, this particular Paul mentored wannabee entrepreneurs. He taught me how to write a plan that would convince a would-be investor why they should part with their cash and invest in a new idea. This is basically what I needed to do at UB a few years later.

So when given the opportunity to set up a digital function in a very traditional UK manufacturing business, although I did not know exactly what to do, I did know exactly where to start.

To get the CEO and wider leadership team on board, I knew there were several aspects to my digital plan that were absolute mandatories: a credible business strategy; a simple way of upskilling the entire organisation on what 'digital' was all about; clarity on where to play and how to win; a new way of engaging the trade; a robust Test and Learn programme.

Into this mix I brought my strong belief of seeing everything through the shopper's eyes: what would make a material difference to the shopper experience in the plethora of information available to help create my plan? So with this in mind, I trawled the web for background information which would be of use, and also tapped into UB's existing agency relationships.

Kantar was the only data provider that produced a trusted online share read so they were used to quantify the opportunity. Insight reports provided good material on the online shopper so they were quoted extensively as well. Publicly available information from Reevoo, Google, Rackspace and others helped fill in the gaps.

At the heart of the plan was the first iteration of The 4 P Framework. The reason for the 4 Ps? Simply because everyone in UB knew the traditional 4 Ps of Marketing, so it seemed like a fairly easy leap for the business to make to understand that we needed a further 4 Ps to crack the digital nut too. And it was!

The first iteration of The 4 P Framework was as follows:

1) Perfect Online Products: ie ensure that the online Point of Purchase (PoP) works as well as it can to influence shoppers to select your products.

2) Partner of Choice: ie ensure that all retailers think of you first when they want to work with a category partner online.

3) Personalised Engagement: ie use tools and techniques to tailor the shopper offer to ensure maximum engagement with your products.

4) Present Everywhere: ie have an 'always on' mentality to ensure that shoppers are always able to buy one of your products to meet their needs.

Or in today's language if you prefer: Fix the Basics; invest in working closely with retailers; unlock the power of data; do what Byron Sharp says. Although I must admit, I just prefer calling this approach The 4 Ps.

This was the framework that I developed to occupy the d-Commerce Box 2 at UB, and the same approach has been used on a number of occasions since then as well. Necessity was absolutely the mother of invention, and it was not long before people around the office and agency partners were talking about The 4 Ps in both urgent and non-urgent important moments alike.

Amazon and D2C 101.

I am just going to come straight out and say it: I have rarely believed there is a priority shopper or business rationale for many CPG brands to go to the potentially considerable cost and effort levels required to list and maintain their products on Amazon, or via a proprietary D2C platform. There may be much easier and more rewarding places to focus on first.

In a small number of product categories: possibly; in smaller brands where their web presence has evolved first through one of these d-Commerce subchannels: definitely. For many brands: focus initially on the Dotcoms (including Ocado) and other d-Commerce subchannels.

The reason I have this view is three-fold:

1) As a lifelong Shopper Marketer, I do not believe that brands can automatically offer a point of interest (or difference) that is motivating enough for a shopper to purchase online *from them* via

Amazon or D2C. This is because shoppers' needs are most likely already being adequately serviced elsewhere. From the business perspective, they are possibly also being serviced more profitably elsewhere too.

Shoppers need a substantive trigger to incentivise a purchase. What is it about your particular brand listing that will make them want to part with their cash whilst shopping on Amazon, or go to the trouble of seeking out your D2C platform?

2) We have conditioned people in the UK to expect a certain kind of shop window when they grocery shop online. With the best will in the world, neither the Amazon platform nor a proprietary brand store currently look, feel or act like what our online shoppers may consider 'normal' from Tesco.com et al.

Of course, shopping on Amazon is great in many ways, and you can have a much different shopping experience from that which you would encounter on the Dotcoms. There is also a lot that we can learn from Amazon's business which is covered further below. For now, I am only making the point that you should perhaps not assume that you need to divert valuable business resources to unlocking Amazon *today*.

It is easy to understand why Amazon want a piece of the UK grocery market. From the shopper's or the brand owner's perspective I am yet to be fully convinced that it should be the top d-Commerce slam dunk for your business.

Remember that your brands are probably already on sale on Amazon, via some industrious Marketplace seller who has purchased them from you at some point. This means that you do already have a presence on the site (which is possibly part of the reason you are considering engaging the company directly anyhow).

But from the shopper's perspective, the vast majority will not know what a Marketplace or direct seller is; they just see your brands. So back to my opening gambit, what exactly *is* the benefit in the grand scheme of things?

Given, there may well be a shonky image or suboptimal product description, and you may lose a brand engagement opportunity as a result. However, in the effort v reward trade off that I am going to explore now, might you not be better expending your precious business resources in another opportunity area first?

3) Setting up and running an Amazon or D2C business offering can take a lot of time and money. You need to be very clear that the venture will bring sufficient payback to make it worthwhile.

When I first looked at a (CEO Pet Project) D2C proposition, there was a point of difference to offer from the shopper's perspective, which even ticked the box of one of the Ps! The idea was to offer shoppers the opportunity to personalise packaging when they ordered the item from a new dedicated brand website. However, on its own, this was in no way even close to dragging the business case past first base.

Even the most optimistic incremental sales opportunity modelling suggested a payback on the set-up investment (platform and supply chain solution) of over seven years; and this was before we even had a meaningful view on how we might tell people about it. It is very difficult for an established brand to make financial sense via a D2C offensive in the UK in my view.

Is there a defensive rationale to launch a branded D2C offer in a category where a disruptor is stealing sales and share with some alacrity? Again, I am not completely convinced, unless you can offer that key point of difference talked about above.

If your brand is being commercially impacted because your previously 'loyal' consumers have found a proposition that better meets their needs, then I think this talks much more to a major brand challenge than it does to a lack of presence in a specific d-Commerce subchannel.

I think we can also apply some of these points to trading with Amazon. When I first looked at setting up a vendor account ten years ago, this was at the time when promises of 'endless aisles', 'first mover advantage' and the Amazon opportunity first appeared in earnest.

For numerous sound reasons, the business I worked at did not engage directly with them at that time, and I believe this was the right decision. With any retailer it is very important to balance potential effort in (eg investment levels, global JBPs, admin overload, access to data) versus reward out (eg sales delivered). Only then can you make an informed decision about the best way to proceed.

In the spirit of balance, there are of course plenty of Amazon advocates and success stories out there: businesses have invested in ensuring that their products look great on the platform; that when shoppers search for their brands they get the one that the brand owner wants them to buy at the top of the list; that when searching for competitor brand terms their shoppers are presented with their own products instead.

These are all sensible decisions made for good reasons, and as I said above, Amazon can work well in some product categories. Just do not assume it has to, or will, work easily in yours.

In summary, be absolutely certain that Amazon and/ or D2C are fairly appraised in relation to the entire melting pot of d-Commerce opportunities before you engage.

Align business resources and sales opportunities.

This may sound obvious, but let us consider for a moment a scenario that is not currently uncommon in many CPG firms: a business with a dedicated Pure Play Account Manager, and no dedicated Dotcom Account Manager.

If this applies to you, then your business is possibly not aligning its business resources with its sales opportunities.

If you look at the Kantar Panel data for your category, then add in something like Amazon PCOGS[4] to get an idea of the total online category size, then the share split will probably look something like:

Tesco: under 50% category sales and dropping; JS, ASDA, Ocado: 10-15% each; Morrisons and Waitrose: 5-10% each; Amazon under 5%, and possibly way under.

So why is it that you have a dedicated Pure Play Account Manager and maybe no one with dedicated focus on the Dotcoms? Possibly due to P&L visibility and responsibility; possibly because someone in the Tesco team can 'pick online up'; possibly as a result your business is not fishing where the biggest fish are.

I will share some thoughts below on a potential evolutionary digital organisational model. For now, let us stay focused on creating the basics and dealing with the current situation.

Your business absolutely needs dedicated d-Commerce resource. Depending on your business's size and scale, you need a minimum of one clued up Account Manager, and ideally a couple with some dedicated d-Category and d-Shopper resource on the side.

I know that resource is not a free-flowing tap in any business, but once you properly model the size of the opportunity, who could in right conscience say no?

We also need to help our d-Commerce team focus on the Healthy Distractions in its day to day work. If you look behind the online scoring in retailer surveys such as the AGS[5], then we get a sense for what the retailers want their online account teams to be doing. This might not be a bad place to start when thinking about your team's focus areas.

The manufacturers that score highly tend to have a few things in common, and interestingly these things also tend to be the ones that the retailers like their suppliers to do for offline as well. These things

---

[4] Measure used by some manufacturers as equivalent to Amazon RSV.
[5] Advantage Group International, *Advantage Group Survey 2018*.

include: appropriate investment; category expertise; tailored support; dedicated account teams. If your business is doing, or can start doing, some of these then you are heading in the right direction.

In the d-Commerce world, we can use our 4 P Framework to identify specific retailer and shopper focused activities that fit well under each of these areas:

Perfect Online Products: ensure clear hi-res pack shots are available in Brandbank with multiple angles and additional Hero information (brand, format, variant, size count) included for mobile; ensure product descriptions are accurate and commonly ubiquitous; have a search strategy in place.

Once these basics are covered, then adapt your offline Purchase Decision Hierarchy for online. Also ensure you have a measurement, management, and optimisation plan in place for your online PoP.

Partner of Choice: understand your retailer's online ambitions, and champion these back into the business; establish eJBPs (online business plans) with dedicated investment for online activity; share best practice with them (or just stuff that you like!) that you have seen elsewhere. This is really all about giving the retailer reasons to want to engage you and your business in addition to Business As Usual (BAU) activities.

On the investment and eJBP question, there are some common investment ratios that I have advised and heard on numerous occasions. For a meaningful Partner of Choice proposition, 6-8% of net customer rev investment is the 'right' number for a 'hold' position; 'grow' should be more like 10-12%.

One relevant caveat: having these investment ratios is one thing; getting the data to understand the state of play today can be more of a challenge.

Personalised Engagement: understand your retailer's approach to data usage and targeting. Where you can, try out some of the customisation options that the retailer offers. Depending on the wider data expertise in your company, ensure your insight team is fully aware of what you are doing and ask them for help if needed.

Present Everywhere: understand the engagement options from the retailer that target shoppers along the Path to Purchase (P2P) on their website. Most of the retailers' media brochures contain some sort of split around 'Consider; Engage; Buy; Repeat' which can help shape your planning.

If you are not clear, then ask your retailer contacts to explain. There are also a host of further pointers in the section on Omnichannel Shopper Marketing Playbooks in Chapter 5.

In the same way that manufacturers have had to work out what to do for themselves over the last few years, so have the retailers. Outside of the day to day trading relationships, there are many retailer employees who see the value of engaging their supplier base to share information and ideas.

You might have to dig around a bit to find them, but I believe most buyers would open the door to the wider business if the day to day relationship is in ok shape. They would be even more likely to do this if you have something they perceive is of value to the wider business. A good, solid d-Commerce strategic framework like The 4 Ps can provide that wider value in my experience.

The final point I want to make in this section about aligning business resources and sales opportunities is regarding an online channel that is becoming increasingly interesting for a number of manufacturers in the UK. This channel is Wholesale (or B2B in d-Commerce speak).

I absolutely advocate starting with the big fish in UK d-Commerce (ie Dotcoms including Ocado) as you should hopefully by now appreciate. Before you move on to d-Commerce opportunity area #2 and dive into Amazon however, it may be worth trying to understand the scale of the online opportunity in B2B. 4 Ps will still work here, just bear in mind that it is the small store owner that we typically need to influence, rather than the end purchaser of the product in store. We will come back to

B2B in Chapter 5.

Data in focus #1: 'Some idiot from Burton's Biscuits'.

Disclaimer alert: to my knowledge, there are no idiots employed at Burton's Biscuits. The reason why I have included this quote here, is because this is what someone said in reaction to the first view on data in d-Commerce that I shared with the world.

In all fairness to him, I think he did not know he was talking about me, to me, when I ended up working with him a few months later. He was, as far as I am aware to this day, just reflecting on a panel discussion in which I had participated about emerging trends in e-Commerce at the IGD Digital Conference in 2013.

He formed this opinion because of what I said about data in response to a question from the audience. The association with Burton's Biscuits was made, I believe, because I (War*Burton*) was introduced whilst working at a *Biscuits* business at the time.

I know he was talking about my comment, because the view that I shared with the world then was that data did not matter in d-Commerce. This is the idiotic comment that he played back to me later.

I would at this point finally like to come out of the closet and publicly own and defend my comment on two fronts:

Firstly, what I actually meant but clearly failed to articulate, was that we should not let our obsession with data become an Unhealthy Distraction, especially when we are just starting to find our d-Commerce feet. Data is *really important* for lots of reasons in any digital dynamic; it is not the only thing, nor indeed the first thing, to think about in my view. The important first things are covered in the section on The 4 Ps above.

Secondly, in the digital world, it really is ok to get some things wrong some of the time. I would even go so far as to say that if you never get things wrong then you are not really trying hard enough.

Jeff Bezos makes a similar point when he says 'you have to be willing to be misunderstood if you're going to innovate', and 'I knew that if I failed I wouldn't regret that, but I knew the one thing that I might regret is not trying'[6]. So hopefully I am in good company.

Having a genuine Test and Learn mentality towards your d-Commerce strategy is absolutely essential, with both of those components being equally important (ie 'Test' and 'Learn').

As an industry we are getting better at 'knowing' what pays back against our digital dollar; we only know this now because of the tests that have been run, evaluated, and repeated in the past. We do not know yet which of the myriad (new) investment options, both retailer-led and otherwise, may become useful future knowledge. We will only create this useful future knowledge via Test and Learn.

When I started running d-Commerce Test and Learns, I was generously provided a four-figure slush fund by the billion-pound business that was employing me at the time. Proudly I managed even with these crumbs to bring some insight and return back to the business (by spending it on a 'Buy it Now' digital media trial, and by acting as an Angel Investor in a new cashback shopping app if you are interested).

This was enough to reassure the business that we were hunting in the right fields, and I believe in year two I may even have been provided with a five-figure fund.

Because I had already oriented the business around the benefit of a 4 P approach, I was repaid in kind with the invaluable business currency of trust[7] in what I was doing. Buy it Now was a great early iteration of Perfect Online Products, and the cashback shopping app fitted nicely into Partner of Choice.

---

[6] Awaken The Greatness Within. "47 Inspirational Jeff Bezos Quotes on Success"; https://awakenthegreatnesswithin.com/47-inspirational-jeff-bezos-quotes-on-success/ (accessed March 20, 2019).
[7] Stephen M R Covey, *The Speed of Trust,* (London, Free Press, 2008).

Whether or not those things would still work now or even fit against the same P is immaterial. The 4 Ps had done the job that was needed at the time, and had given me the required breathing space to operate.

Another related point here concerns the importance of *learning*. Always ask yourself 'how will I know whether this test has worked or not?'. If you can get a nice clean read on sales payback then that is ideal; if not there are other suitable success measures that you can think about which we will come back to in Chapter 3.

Be clear on what you are trying to achieve, be clear on what success looks like, and then be clear on whether success happened or not. Always Test and Learn; which brings us nicely back to the Damoclean crowdsourced opinion forum of the IGD conference.

This actually represented the culmination of another couple of Test and Learns that had been bubbling away over the preceding few months. In the true retailer engaging spirit of Partner of Choice, I had also tabled two other digital mnemonics with the customer base in the period prior to the conference: 'The P.R.I.C.E. is Right' approach to Connected Retail, and 'The New Ten Commandments' of unlocking social.

Clearly before its time, 'PRICE' described the five 'Shopper Experience' mandatories to focus on when bringing together online and offline to create seamless shopper engagement. This shopper imperative will be returned to later.

Despite sharing some Pure Play offline store concept boards with someone very senior at Ocado, PRICE did not get sufficient traction to move past 'nice idea but' stage. As a result, I sent the boards to my mate Jeff at Amazon and they launched Amazon Go (ok that last bit is a blatant lie). The New Ten Commandments never really got out of the blocks.

The relevance of this to the IGD conference and the Test and Learn principle, is that I included both of these concepts alongside The 4 Ps in my conference presentation. I genuinely wanted to gauge audience reaction, and sought and received feedback from some trusted confidants in that audience afterwards as well. The result: PRICE and The New Ten Commandments went no further, and The 4 Ps did.

Never be afraid to put yourself or what you think out there in the d-Commerce world. The principle of Test and Learn is so integral to how anything digital evolves that without it the pace of development would be significantly curtailed. Whether it is a product iteration in Scrum, a new media test with a retail partner, or just an idea that you want to bounce off someone, just go for it!

And if you are still unsure, check out Google Graveyard, the Amazon Fire Phone, the Apple Pippin or Facebook Places to be reassured that the big boys do not always get it right either.

Creating The Basics in byte sized chunks.

- Create and own a Basics Focus in your business.
- Spend as much time as you can in Box 2.
- Be wary of Unhealthy Distractions.
- Shoppers will not engage with your products if there is nothing in it for them.
- Fish where the fish are. Do not assume they like swimming in the Amazon the most.
- Introduce a simple strategic framework into your business to guide your d-Commerce efforts.
- Appraise all your d-Commerce business subchannel opportunities and align your business resources with sales potential.
- Find a way to give your d-Commerce team freedom to operate.
- Run Test and Learns. Always have an idea of what success looks like.
- Get your ideas out there and see which ones stick. Do not be afraid of failure as you will be in good company.

CHAPTER 2. CHANGE DOESN'T HAVE TO BE CHALLENGING

The Myth of Transformation.

S O WITH 'LEVEL 1 Shields' d-Commerce protection in place, I began the second part of my digital learning journey at a very different business to the first. This time I also had a team, a digitally competent Line Manager, and a more respectable (ie more zeros) Test and Learn budget.

What I also had was the opportunity to take the helm at the Business Unit's 'Digital Transformation' initiative; one of several that had been identified as strategically important by some Big Name Consultants (BNCs) just before I came on board. I was, as I explained to the HR Director during a workshop, 'happy as a pig in muck'.

At this juncture, I think that it is worth questioning what 'Digital Transformation' actually means. Digital Transformation is something that a lot of businesses seem to talk about, and some claim to be doing it. A few have definitely spent lots of money trying it, and at least one or two have brought in more 'operational' folk to actually work out what to do on the ground when those potentially ethereal BNCs have gone home.

Digital Transformation is clearly describing some kind of change programme. It will probably involve some IT stuff, some data stuff, some training stuff and some other stuff; but is Digital Transformation what many CPG business actually need?

My personal view is that many CPG firms need 'Digital Simplification' and not Digital Transformation. Commercially, this may also mean that there are some significant consulting fees to be saved by not too quickly subscribing to a potentially over-promising sales pitch. To keep the Bezos quote theme going, those BNCs categorically 'see your margin as their opportunity'[8] here.

I believe that we are in danger of subscribing to 'The Myth of (Digital) Transformation' which can be articulated as follows:

Digital Transformation has become synonymous with a unicorn-like panacea that will address all business ills, whilst simultaneously unlocking a new stratosphere bound commercial trajectory. Unfortunately, unicorn-like panaceas just do not exist.

Has Digital Transformation become a bit of a BNC inspired misnomer, when what people really need is just some help understanding the digital world and what to do about it? My experience suggests sometimes maybe it is.

A lot of those BNCs have struggled to work out what to do in the digital world just as much as we have over the last few years. Buoyed by success in other data rich and IT literate verticals such as Financial Services, however, the BNCs have genuinely seen a new revenue waterfall from unlocking Digital Transformation (DT) in CPG. I am sure some good projects have been delivered in this vein; I just have not heard about many yet.

---

[8] Ibid.

The key point is that CPG is genetically different from those other verticals with regard to two essential pillars of a DT programme: IT infrastructure and data. If your business genuinely has the appetite and wallet to embark on the BNC 'Lift and Drop' DT plan then I wish you the best of luck; just proceed with caution.

Do not get me wrong. As already stated I am a big believer in sharing learning and experience in the digital world. Since my early days on ISBA's[9] Digital Action Group, I have vociferously stated that 'digital' is the one part of business where knowledge and learning can most easily cross vertical boundaries.

My only counsel here is to think very carefully about what kind of shared learning will benefit your business the most on the d-Commerce (or digital more widely) ticket. It is unlikely to be IT or data infrastructure in my view. You do not need to reach for the six (or seven!) figure electronic chequebook to start realising some significant d-Commerce upsides.

So in the spirit of Digital Simplification, here are some things that you could consider doing first:

1) Appoint a specialist focused team whose sole reason for being on this planet is to lead the Simplification programme. Could be external, could just as well be internal; needs to have full leadership sponsorship and be fairly digitally switched on either way.

2) Seek and gain agreement to definition and expectations of the Simplification up front. Spend time defining what key stakeholders in the business think, or want Digital Simplification to deliver. I think you will be surprised, and I can completely endorse this as the right approach thanks to bitter experience of its antithesis.

3) Set out and follow a structured change journey. Again, I do not believe that you need to spend a lot of money on BNCs to bring this

---

[9] The Incorporated Society of British Advertisers.

to life in your business. Read some very accessible Kotter[10] for some tips, or apply existing company best practice. Only then if you are not sure, ask for some help.

And most importantly of all...

4) Deploy a simple strategic framework that everyone in your business can quickly grasp, and enables them to understand exactly what to focus on to win in the digital world; which, conveniently, is where The 4 P Framework nicely fits in. When I deployed this at the heart of a digital change programme, The 4 Ps actually became 5 Ps, and the rationale and methodology followed is covered in more detail below.

For now though, it is just worth making the point, that what The Ps actually stand for is in some ways secondary to the Box 2 benefit that they may have in your business. By cutting right through the myriad layers of potential digital complexity that now constitute our world, The Ps quickly enable everyone in the business to feel comfortable with the *digital* world. Then the lightbulb moments begin.

In the same way that the traditional 4 Ps of Marketing shape what we do to make our brands accessible, think about the digital Ps as being the business lubrication that you need to make the Digital Simplification magic start to happen.

Do not assume that you need a significant transformation programme to 'get digital'. Take a breath and put your best foot forwards. There is already a great deal of good knowledge and practice in the traditional (ie non-digital) way of doing business that can be just as effective, with only minor modifications, in the digital world too.

Work with what you've got.

So what have you already got in your business that can help crack the d-

---

[10] John P Kotter, *Leading Change*, (USA, HBS Press, 1996).

Commerce nut? I imagine amongst other things you have a team of talented individuals, an opportunity to sell more in the fastest growing CPG sales channel[11], and possibly a desire to 'do more with digital' as part of your overall business approach. This desire to 'do more with digital' may have been called out internally, or was maybe articulated with the help of some of those BNCs I ranted a bit about above.

You also have a team of people who are comfortably using social media, Amazon, apps etc in their personal lives, but may have not yet made the connection to how these things can help unlock business performance too. If you have some or all of these things then you have definitely got enough to get started with Digital Simplification.

A useful technique that I have deployed to kick off a Digital Simplification workstream workshop, involves setting the attendees a very simple pre-work task. Running successful workshops is all about delegate participation, and so it helps to get them talking and sharing from the start.

What I asked the delegates to do, was to think about one piece of digital content that they liked. This could be a website, app, video or whatever, and could be work related or non-work related. The delegates had to come to the workshop prepared to share their content, and explain what they liked about it. I set this pre-work task for a couple of reasons.

As already highlighted, it really helps run a successful workshop if you get people participating from the start, and there are of course a number of means by which this can be accomplished. What I wanted to do additionally here though, was get some common recognition and agreement that there is much more that brings us together on a Digital Simplification ticket than divides us. Allow me to explain.

Everybody has a favourite video, website or app that they use on a regular basis, or have proudly shared with their friends at some point in

---

[11] IGD. "UK Channel Opportunities 2018-2023";
https://retailanalysis.igd.com/Portals/1/Downloads/UK-Channel-Opportunities-2018-23-webinar.pdf (accessed March 20, 2019).

the past. It could be a funny video, a really neat life enhancing 'wow' thingy or even Tinder (which has come up more than once!). What it is does not matter. The key point is that we are already all 'doing digital' in our lives as I pointed out above.

The magic starts to happen when people start to explain why they like this particular piece of content: it is funny; it simplifies their lives; it is really clever; it looks good; they have a great returns policy (possibly that last one does not relate to Tinder). Hopefully you get the gist. And it is not a big leap from this kind of exercise to highlight that people are talking about Personalisation, Perfect Online Products, Present Everywhere etc.

Without realising it, the delegates have started to explain what works for them in the digital world amongst a group of their trusted peers. And if it works for them in their personal lives, then why could it not work for their wider business approach too?

When I started to introduce the idea of The 4 Ps into a different business from the one of its genesis, I remember feeling a certain amount of trepidation. First time around, The 4 Ps had been carefully constructed, carefully embedded, and importantly I had also developed the trust that is so important when a business is venturing into a new area.

This time I was the new kid on the block, the business I was in was already very credibly established in the digital space, and there was definitely a higher bar and deeper pool of digital knowledge in the business than I was used to. Gulp.

So in the true spirit of Test and Learn, I just thought 'let's go for it', and chucked the idea of a similar business unifying digital framework into an international workshop. And it was well received.

Interestingly though, it was the idea of The 4 Ps that resonated the most, rather than the actual definition of what each P stood for or talked about. Focus on areas like Personalisation was met with quick agreement and support, but was Present Everywhere really what we wanted to achieve with our Marketing Strategy? Not sure. To be honest,

I was genuinely just a bit chuffed that I had added some value to my new employer; the fact that the room was full of quite senior folk had nothing to do with it.

From this I took an important learning that is very relevant to this wider idea of working with what you have got: you need to flex your approach a bit and bring people with you on any kind of Simplification journey.

'One Size Fits All' does not always work well in CPG, as every business has its own unique strengths and challenges. A top down push of a set framework will have no lasting impact when the pusher goes home or moves on; you have to help the business develop from within. This is particularly pertinent for Digital Simplification.

So once the workstream attendees have agreed that in the digital world there is more that unites than divides us, there is a good common base from which to move forwards. By starting to pull out some common threads of focus, you can then move on as a unified group to think about what all this means for business strategy.

Following this approach makes it possible to determine an alternative iteration of the 4 Ps (or 5 Ps) which may look something like:

1) Perfect User Interface: ie ensure your business's user interfaces work as effectively as possible. Apply Perfection to all the points of interaction between your business users and your company.

2) Personalised Experiences: ie use data to engage with your business users in value additive and relevant ways. Derive tangible commercial benefit via deployment of a data strategy that works.

3) Present Where and When Relevant: ie make sure that your shoppers can engage with your products wherever or whenever there is an appropriate opportunity to do so (for them or your business).

4) Pre-empt the Future: ie be on the front foot to identity and engage with the best Test and Learn opportunities as they come along. Have an agreed framework for quickly assessing and funding those

opportunities.

5) Pursue Meaningful Engagement: ie use appropriate digital means to engage all business stakeholders in online dialogue.

There are pros and cons of the definition process and content of both the 4 P and 5 P Frameworks covered above. What would however be common to both, are the lightbulb moments that happen when employees grasp the demystifying power contained therein. Businesses may start to feel that they know what to focus on to win in the digital world, and feel much more comfortable with what they are talking about. And all of this without the cost, complexity and confusion of a full BNC DT programme.

One of the positive things about a crowdsourced 5 P Framework, is regarding what can happen after its inception. If you work with a cross functional team and follow the Kotter inspired[12] roadmap below, then after signing off The Framework at step 3, it is possible to collectively translate The Ps into what they mean for different business functions.

Figure 2: Digital Simplification roadmap.

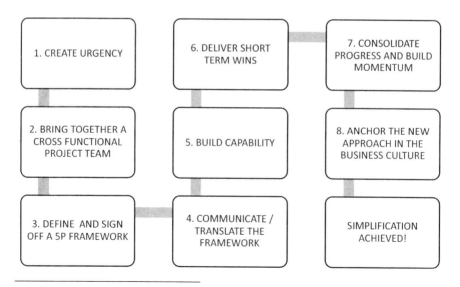

---

[12] Kotter, *Leading Change.*

This means that the workstream moves on to more of a 'what does it mean for me?' type focus. For all business functions, you can identify a project or job to be done that is relevant under each P. I have seen this work with 5 Ps and 5 business functions, where an action plan known as the '5 by 5' was born. More simplification, more clarity, more focus.

The final point to make in this section also fits neatly under the 'working with what you've got' banner. Cross business workshops with a proper pre and post work plan are fundamental to the momentum and success of any business change initiative. A successful workshop programme that your business is proud of and the delegates rave about will only help garner support of both the 'hearts and minds' of your people. Both hearts and minds need to be on board to reap the biggest rewards of any new wider digital, or more function specific d-Commerce, approach.

People expect digital to be fun and interesting and it is. They also expect it to be a bit new and scary which it can be sometimes. To simultaneously recognise and deliver against this, I would strongly recommend the following simple mantra to shape all workshop and alignment meetings: 'Inspire; Simplify; Educate'.

Start each session with something Inspirational: share some cool content or bring in a speaker if there is practical scope to do so. Follow this with something Simple or Simplifying: pick a P or a few Ps if you want. Then Educate: what does all this mean and what needs to be done about it?

Winning hearts and minds is of paramount importance for delivering any major business initiative, and this is definitely true for Digital Simplification. For Digital Simplification to work, there are some additional specific considerations that it might be worth making as well. These concern the different needs and expectations of disparate groups of people in your business, and of one group in particular.

The Marzipan Layer.

If you lay out a clear roadmap, and devote and deliver appropriate levels of Inspiration, Simplification and Education to its realisation, then you will be making a solid start down the path of Digital Simplification glory. Bring the business with you through sensible management of your workshops and workstreams, and you will happily trudge a couple more steps along. Change does not always have to be challenging; sometimes however it can be.

I cannot remember the first time I heard the term 'Marzipan Layer' and I am not claiming to be its originator. I like to think I am one of its keenest proponents however, in terms of understanding and addressing its potential Digital Simplification impact.

The Marzipan Layer in a business refers to that group of people, typically senior managers, that sit between the Fruit Cake (the foot soldiers) and the C-Suite (the Icing, naturally). All three elements are necessary to the successful construction and operation of any business cake, and all three can have a different impact and effect on the business via their actions.

The Marzipan Layer deservedly occupies an exalted position in business. The employees therein have demonstrated the leadership skills and necessary expertise to garner the business's trust. The Layer constitutes a diverse range of skills and backgrounds, and it is crucial to get the Marzipan Layer on board in its entirety for Digital Simplification to work.

The key point here, is that when it comes to 'digital', the Marzipan Layer's diversity in skills and backgrounds can be quite pronounced. This diversity may be less pronounced in either the Fruit Cake or the Icing, possibly due to demographic reasons. From the point of view of Digital Simplification, elements of the Marzipan Layer may therefore need special consideration.

The foot soldiers constitute the day to day 'doers' of the business. Those employees, more likely junior in the business hierarchy, that are responsible for the BAU customer interaction, brand management, reporting etc. All very important tasks and essential to smooth business operation.

What is particularly relevant here, however, is that the foot soldiers typically tend to be Generation Y (or Millennials) born from 1981 onwards[13]. This means that many foot soldiers cannot immediately relate to 'more traditional' content that includes pictures of cassette tapes with pencils and the like.

What they can relate to much more easily are the content and products of the 'Digital Revolution'. The Digital Revolution started in earnest in the 1990s during Gen Y's most formative years. Consequently, many foot soldiers have grown up with smartphones, Social Media, You Tube etc and it 'just is' part of their normal life.

For most Generation Xers (born between 1965 and 1980[14]), and many CPG companies of equivalent vintage, 'digital' *is* something a bit newer and scarier that needs to be reconciled. With the usual generation generalisation disclaimers applied, 'digital' is not something that 'just is' for Gen X. And Gen X can be a dominant demographic in the Marzipan Layer.

For the Icing, they know that something needs to be done about the Digital Revolution in order to make their businesses fit for the future: new sales channels are opening up and new ways of engaging consumers and shoppers are appearing. 'Digital' will, without necessarily needing to know exactly how, continue to fundamentally impact the Icing's top and bottom lines. So the Icing is all for it, without really needing to know much of the detail.

What this creates is an interesting and understandable dynamic in some businesses. The Fruit Cake and the Icing are very interested in doing some good digital stuff, although possibly for slightly different reasons: digital makes the foot soldiers' world go round, and digital will mean the C-Suite's business wheels will continue to turn in the future.

However, through no fault of their own, some of the Marzipan Layer

---

[13] Wikipedia. "Millennials"; https://en.wikipedia.org/wiki/Millennials (accessed March 20, 2019).

[14] Wikipedia. "Generation X"; https://en.wikipedia.org/wiki/Generation_X (accessed March 20, 2019).

may be in the position where they just do not quite 'get digital' enough to feel comfortable. Due to the expectations coming top down and bottom up, this discomfort has to be addressed and may manifest itself in a number of ways.

Starting with the positives, some of those in the Marzipan Layer lacking the requisite digital knowledge will quite readily recognise this understandable gap. Consequently, they will hire, build, and support capability to plug it into their team.

Some of the Marzipan Layer, however, may feel particularly uncomfortable as a result of this business dynamic. This can result in a number of behaviours ranging from the Ostrich (head in the sand), to the Roadrunner (too busy to stop and think), to the Thor's Hammer (Smash. You just cannot do that). These behaviours can all have a detrimental impact on a Digital Simplification initiative.

But remember that for this part of the Marzipan Layer, it is not of their making. It 'just is'. This knowledge gap is merely a function of what was happening in the wider environment during their formative years. As custodians of our Digital Simplification ambitions, we must therefore find a workable way of resolving this dynamic.

If simple appeals to better nature fall on deaf ears, then it may be worth fostering involvement in some 'Shiny Things'. Shiny Things are those high impact digital things essential for BAU. Importantly they are also very accessible, which means that a diverse group of employees can contribute without the need for specialist digital knowledge. This 'hands on' participation, perhaps coupled with targeted Capability Development, may go some way to helping parts of the Marzipan Layer feel more comfortable.

A couple of Shiny Things you might want to try could be:

1) Establishing a 'Digital Packaging' workflow or charter. Your marketing department is, hopefully, all over the primary physical packaging that surrounds your lovely products in the local Tesco store. In the same way Marketing need to own the primary Digital

Packaging too: the pack images; the product information; the back of pack detail. This is marketing bread and butter and is good Level 1 Perfect Online Products, and something that cannot happen without marketing sign off.

You can also extend this to providing Hero pack information as well. Just show your business how insignificant its products can look on Dotcom mobile if more convincing is required.

2) Conducting a Shopper Experience (SX) review. More on this in Chapter 5, but take a screen grab of how one of your products is showing up *really badly* on a retailer website, then share it along with some thoughts on how this could be fixed. Many businesses do not have to look too far to find a *really bad* example (check B2B if Dotcom is ok), and even tag on some hilarious online review to really Thor's Hammer the point home. Politely ask your senior leader if they would be happy if the product was showing up like this in store.

3) Create a list of sensible search terms that will apply for both a Marketing Google keyword strategy as well as a Sales one for a retailer site. Ask your Marzipan Layer to contribute to and endorse it.

At a basic level, creating a keyword strategy is something anyone can do and you do not need agency help to do this. Agree the answers to these three questions to get started:

-   What category terms do you want your brand to be associated with?
-   What brand terms do you want your brand to be associated with?
-   What complementary products do you want your brand to be associated with?

Go through this process and you will have about 10-15 keywords on your list. Level 1 keyword strategy complete.

There are of course other more strategic ways to properly engage the Marzipan Layer and help them feel more comfortable: a properly executed 4 P or 5 P Digital Simplification programme is certainly one way. Notwithstanding that, it may also be worth trying some of the tactical suggestions above.

The right kind of partners.

There are, as I hope you are starting to appreciate, a few different things that you can do to start decoding d-Commerce in your business right now. Many of these can be done with some focused effort and without need for external expertise. If the need for external expertise does arise, then it is crucial that the right kind of partners are brought in to maximise your chances of success.

A new approach; some new thinking; an agile mentality: all of these will benefit your business no end as it travels down the d-Commerce path. It is therefore essential that your external partners are also able to deliver these kinds of d-Success prerequisites.

In d-Marketing, for example, the shockwaves being sent through the agency world are well documented. Agencies are facing a transparency and talent crisis caused by the evolving (digital) needs of the marketing department[15].

In Sales, we have a different agency model to that of our Marketing brethren. However, we need to be just as aware of the same destabilising impact of the new digital world order.

One area popular for sourcing external support in Sales is in creation of a Category Vision (or Category Strategy as it is sometimes called). As essential fuel to underpin retailer engagement for many CPG firms, it is crucial that your Category Vision (CV) is fit for d-Commerce purpose on numerous levels. There is possibly a chance that it is not.

---

[15] The Drum. "Agencies aren't just facing a talent crisis – they're in danger of terminal decline"; https://www.thedrum.com/opinion/2018/10/25/agencies-arent-just-facing-talent-crisis-they-re-danger-terminal-decline (accessed 20 March, 2019).

As is the case with other 'old world' thinking, many CVs are created using a process that was devised in the 1990s, and has basically been rolled on in various iterations ever since. But how many of these CVs are having the effect that the commissioners want them to, or were maybe promised when the CV was crafted in the first instance?

At the coalface of omnichannel shopper engagement, I do not believe that many manufacturers can honestly say that their CV is making a material difference either online or in store. CV execution is generally speaking very poor, and this is possibly due to one of the following reasons:

1) A CV no longer gives a point of difference in its own right. Every credible category player has one now, and they all talk to broadly the same things (convenience, health, premiumisation, new occasions anyone?). As a result, they are losing their 'Wow Factor' with the trade.

2) Businesses have, for whatever reason, invested their efforts in the CV 'Build' without thinking as much about the other two crucial elements: 'Embed' and 'Execute'. In an industry where the shopper is king, this is just not good enough.

3) Because of 1) and 2), a lot of CVs are just a bit flat and tired.

The 'tried and tested' method of CV creation has become 'tired and vested'. The agencies that produce the CVs in this way have a vested interest in keeping on doing the same thing, because why would they not? The fees are still coming in and there is always a new market or supplier rehash to go after. There is a lot of process waste, inefficient working, and as we have already highlighted, suboptimal execution.

This is the exact same backdrop that led to the emergence of Scrum in the Software Development industry in the 1990s: projects were inefficiently managed, execution was poor and the whole sorry experience was too process heavy. That industry changed its approach and I think we can all probably agree has done rather well as a result.

Surely then there is an argument to apply the same overhaul to the CV development process? Or indeed any process where external input is required to support your Omnichannel Strategy. Do not expect to do the same thing in the same way and get a different result.

If a 'Category Vision Scrum' all sounds a bit heavy or impractical, then I would endorse a Shiny Thing approach here as well. There are a great number of Shiny Things that can be done to bring your existing CV or d-Commerce strategy to life: apps, websites, nicely designed interactive PDFs to name a few. Roll in your Scrum-ptious brand new omnichannel-shopper-centric-CV and you might then have a really impressive Shiny Thing.

Only work with partners that can provide these kinds of solutions for your business. If you do, the overall impact will be increased nicely.

Data in focus #2: The wrong way to address Digital Capability.

Think very carefully before agreeing to cover a conference presentation for someone if you are not 100% clued up on audience expectations.

Just in terms of context, a very capable d-Commerce person who once worked in my team asked me at short notice to cover a conference presentation for him at the Festival of Marketing in 2017. He claimed he was ill, and knowing well of my incessant passion to talk about what I think on contemporary digital subjects, asked me to cover for him.

The subject was the new European data regulations known as The General Data Protection Regulation or GDPR, and I agreed to do it without much of a second thought.

Despite Project Fear type speculation about its impact, when GDPR landed in May 2018 it was in many ways a bit of a damp squib. Some folk (myself included) took it as an opportunity to clear out which electronic mailing lists they were signed up to; others got a bit sick and tired of the tsunami of (unnecessary) validation emails being sent out by anyone with a database, and gave up after answering one or two.

GDPR at the time was a really big deal. It kind of came along in 2017 and no one really knew about it, which sent the industry into proper panic mode. A whole cottage industry sprang up to deal with the whole cottage industry, and it was definitely a hot topic at the Festival of Marketing in 2017.

Despite knowing the GDPR basics, I assumed that the conference audience would derive more benefit from some pointers on how to help their businesses improve its overall Digital Capability, including readiness for things like GDPR. I should have remembered that adage that was common parlance in the business where I spent my formative CPG years and 'never assumed'.

The presentation went really badly, and this was categorically the wrong way to address Digital Capability.

So for the benefit of the disappointed delegates who may have missed the key points of my presentation in their 'lack of expected subject matter' disgust, I am going to have another go now. There is definitely a right way to build Digital Capability in your business.

'We need to raise our Digital Capability!'; 'We need more digital expertise!'; 'We need digital training!'. Sound familiar? Chances are somewhere in your organisation these or similar rallying cries have sounded out in recent times. So just find some decent trainers, recruit some talent, or license some handily packaged solutions. Right way? No, wrong way again.

For me, the secret to building Digital Capability lies in the principle of Simon Sinek's Golden Circles[16]: start with the 'why', then think about the 'how', and only then focus on the 'what' (ie the best training solution).

Or in other words: do not jump in and just commission a new training solution, without carefully thinking through 'how' it will be delivered and embedded in your organisation. Do not do this without starting off

---

[16] Simon Sinek, *Start With Why: How Great Leaders Inspire Everyone To Take Action*, (Penguin, UK, 2009).

with a clearly understood and aligned 'why' it is needed in the first place.

Many businesses may have the wrong approach to Digital Capability (or capability more generally). They may waste their hard-earned cash on programmes that have little relevance to current business challenges, and have little impact before and after the programme is delivered. This kind of organisational profligacy can give training a bad name. The reason some businesses may do this could be simply because they do not understand the core point of the preceding two paragraphs.

So in the spirit of applying Sinek's model to the area of Digital Capability, start off by asking: 'Why does my organisation need to improve its Digital Capability?'. Some possible answers might be:

1) Because your business is underperforming v competitors in key digital channels.

2) Because your business wants to engage shoppers or consumers through digital channels more effectively.

3) Because some of your senior leaders are a bit almond (marzipan) flavoured when it comes to 'digital', and you hope some training will nudge them fully into the 21st century (remember it is not their fault).

4) Because you know that decent Capability Development is the lifeblood of any business, driving employee retention and competitive advantage.

By clearly articulating the 'why', it is then easier to move on to think about 'how' your business can address its Digital Capability. Some good things to include might be:

- 'Learning Journey' principles in place.
- '70:20:10' principles in place.
- Competency levels understood and properly benchmarked.
- Line Manager support in place.
- Objectives aligned and understood.

- Triple lock budget in place.

And when you have worked through both the 'why' and the 'how', only then move on to work out 'what' blended solutions should be delivered into your business. Only at this point, if it is necessary, reach for the electronic chequebook.

In addition to 'because Simon says so', there is another very valid reason to address Digital Capability in this way:

Businesses have different cultures and needs when it comes to building any kind of capability, and especially so in the new-fangled world of d-Commerce. There is not a One Size Fits All solution to improve Digital Capability in your business. Many businesses have bought into nicely packaged e-Learning based solutions; some are even still using them after the initial three-line-whip box ticking exercise came to an end. Or actually, are they?

Remember that your Fruit Cake, Marzipan Layer and Icing all have different levels of knowledge, different requirements, and different levels of engagement with the digital world. Even within these groups there may be a need for some kind of tiered solution that brings in 'Foundation', 'Intermediate' and 'Advanced' options.

Only when you are absolutely clear on the above points should you think about learning apps, e-Learning modules, webinars, workshop-based solutions, business games, coaching or whatever combination is right for you and your employees. These should then be tailored for your business to deliver your specific objectives, rather than something 'off the peg'.

When it comes to capability, your business cannot 'go digital' overnight, or even over-year for that matter. Unless it is some wonderfully Agile, genuinely flexible, bureaucratically light anti-behemoth of a very funky place to work then you are going to need more than a simple training solution; but do not worry you are not alone.

Like I was on that Festival of Marketing stage.

—

Change Doesn't Have To Be Challenging in byte sized chunks.

- Think carefully if you need Digital Transformation or Digital Simplification.
- Follow a structured roadmap to deliver your change ambitions that is easily accessible to all.
- Be prepared to flex your approach to win your employees' hearts and minds.
- Tap into your employees' existing passion for the digital world around them.
- Think carefully about the needs of the Marzipan Layer.
- Do Shiny Things.
- Choose your partners carefully; there is a chance they might not be able to deliver what your business needs.
- Do not apply old thinking to new opportunities.
- Addressing Digital Capability in the right way is crucial. Think carefully about the 'why' and the 'how' before paying for the 'what'.

CHAPTER 3. ROLL YOUR SLEEVES UP

Nowhere to hide.

THERE IS A very important yin to the wonderful world of strategic 4 or 5 P yang: in order to properly decode d-Commerce, you must absolutely roll your sleeves up and just get stuck in at some point. You need to be 100% accountable for the make or break of your d-Commerce business, because this is the only way you will really learn what will help you swim rather than sink.

Remember that for a lot the Wild West d-Commerce world, there are simply not yet a plethora of widely established best practice or knowledgeable Line Managers to help you out.

By spending a year heading up Digital and Trade Marketing at a seriously cool SME (Small and Medium-sized Enterprise) since bought by Unilever, I was fortunate enough to be able to roll my sleeves so far up, that they pretty much stopped being sleeves and turned into a rather fetching herbal ruff.

Big CPG business and working in big CPG business absolutely have their advantages: working with successful well-known brands; having more clout and airtime with the retailers; personal development and reward;

good people to name but a few. For some though, it also has the advantage of providing a safe place to hide.

Those very things that make big company wheels turn slowly can provide opportunities for some employees to eschew accountability: the upwards delegation; the decision by committee at the decision committee; the endless 'alignment' meetings. These are all accessible shadows where some employees can keep out of the spotlight. Big businesses that foster more agile approaches are starting to shed some of these self-limiting practices.

When a key part of d-Commerce success is literally just getting out there and trying stuff, and sometimes getting things wrong, this approach is not always the best bedfellow for potentially risk-averse big business culture. There are no such hiding places in a successful SME, where sweating assets takes on a whole new meaning. There is much more accountability, and this is a better mindset to model if we want to win in d-Commerce.

In SMEs, the volume of work, the pace of growth, the never-ending list of opportunities to explore (and even sometimes evaluate) all make for a very different culture and working week to that experienced in a bigger business. In bigger businesses the established processes and hierarchies can provide both a safety net and well-oiled brakes. The SME approach to brakes and safety nets is what you might refer to as 'more Victorian'.

Without functional silos, working in SMEs can give you a much healthier view about how digital transcends business functions. In a similar vein you can also develop a more pragmatic perspective on omnichannel shopping behaviour: how shoppers move in and out of on and offline on the way to purchasing a product.

Big businesses apply a multi-channel lens to their commercial approach for sensible business reasons. However, if you just apply the multi-channel filters then you may miss part of the bigger picture.

Through the multi-channel lens, you will see an online channel that accounts for probably between five and ten per cent of your total company sales, with plenty of organic growth left in it. Possible conclusion: 'Yes online is important, but it is growing and I have got more Urgent Important Box 1 pressures over here to think about thanks'.

However, this is only showing part of the picture.

From the P&L perspective, although online might only account for single digit revenue contribution, it may well account for much more than single digit growth contribution.

Even more importantly, how much of your offline purchasing is influenced in some way by what your shoppers see and experience online? There is no definitive number here, but for your category assume it is between thirty and fifty per cent[17] because it will be.

And if you prefer the 'motivation by way of fear' approach, then I can reliably inform you that I know of more than one significant CPG business which has declined online in one or more customers in recent years. That is right, declined online.

The fact that it is possible for even big business to decline sales online should serve as a dire warning to us all. Growth is not guaranteed online forever, and we should not rest on our online growth laurels. Put another way, do not self-limit your perspective of online growth potential due to a linear channel focus. Adopt a shopper first mindset to avoid missing the bigger picture.

It is not the online channel or omnichannel shopper that will be the Achilles Heel in your company growth trajectory, but rather one of your own making. The least bad thing you can do is not plan to do anything about it and assume that online will 'just work'; the worst thing you can do is self-sabotage by applying old business thinking to the new business reality.

---

[17] Industry insight and verbatim.

The SME model provides us a great insight into how we can all manage d-Commerce to win. Ensure a fully autonomous (and therefore fully accountable) d-Commerce person or team features prominently near the start your d-Commerce journey.

Nothing flows through businesses faster than the river of success. It is time to take the shackles off and see how fast your d-Commerce river can flow. The right resource will love having nowhere to hide, and will bring the most benefit to your business too.

D2C 2: The rise of the shopper.

Not an attempt at a suggestion for the name of the latest Star Wars release, but rather a significant underlying industry trend that I think D2C is helping to shine a light on.

As I explained above, D2C is not something that your business should just lurch towards because it seems like a good idea on some level. The number of established CPG brands that could easily make a commercially additive move into this most proprietarily digital of all d-Commerce subchannels is very small.

With no clear shopper or category benefit, the best you are likely to achieve from D2C is some sales steal from a different d-Commerce subchannel. The worst is some kind of super-massive business black hole that will just sap resource, cash, and the souls of all those involved.

This is not necessarily the case for some of those SMEs that have evolved a successful D2C platform as part of their total offering, or are indeed D2C natives. Where D2C has evolved alongside the business to be a core part of the business offer, or even its sole sales channel, then of course it needs to be properly managed, measured and optimised. For most established CPG brands, however, there are quite likely much bigger fish to catch elsewhere first.

For some significant global CPGs, the effect that D2C businesses are having on their megabrands is worthy of note. There has been much observation of the likes of P&G 'being nibbled to death'[18] by smaller players that are tipping the whole notion of brand engagement on its head. The D2Cs are doing this because they are stealing brand share and consumers from the blue-chip behemoths, by quite frankly better addressing a consumer need than the big boys are.

One need only look at Dollar Shave Club to see how this phenomenon has affected two of the titans of the CPG world. It is estimated that the D2C razor blades subchannel has taken $400m out of the US blades market[19], and a lot of this has been at the expense of P&G's flagship blades brand Gillette.

Furthermore, Unilever purchased Dollar Shave Club in 2016 for the spritely sum of $1bn. Clearly there are a number of reasons behind such an acquisition, not least because it enabled Unilever to firmly park a tank on their global rival P&G's lawn. Another reason though, is that the purchase enabled Unilever to learn about the D2C phenomenon from one of the pioneering D2C success stories.

Just in case you do not have $1bn to spend on a similar learning exercise, then I think we can all learn something else of equal importance here. The learning that we can take from D2C is around how this is a proxy for a much deeper question we should all be asking ourselves: which part of CPG, or maybe less pointedly which philosophy, should 'lead' your business to make it most fit for the future?

'We are brand led!' is the traditional view of CPG, and I agree that traditionally this was the case. CPG was all about the brand (there is even a clue in the initialism by the inclusion of 'C'), and this is a legacy position that still endures. But is this actually now harming your business? It may be worth considering that possibly it is.

---

[18] Forbes. "Why Unilever, General Mills And Proctor & Gamble Aren't Good At Marketing In The Modern Economy";
https://www.forbes.com/sites/kimberlywhitler/2018/04/26/why-unilever-general-mills-and-procter-and-gamble-arent-good-at-marketing-in-the-modern-economy/#2038c27616a4 (accessed March 20, 2019).
[19] Industry source.

The whole marketing ethos is currently subject to sensible debate, largely thanks to Byron Sharp[20]. One of my favourite notions in his book is referenced on the back cover, and juxtaposes the traditional concept of marketing to the business parallel of medieval bloodletting. I am not going to attempt to critique Byron Sharp's empirical argument here, because quite frankly he knows much more about it than me; I will however borrow and endorse his wider notion that marketing needs to change.

But why? I think this can be answered with three simple words. At its most base level, the reason why D2C has taken off, and the reason why marketing needs a good old shake up, is because one thing is more important than anything else in today's CPG d-Commerce world: making things *easy to buy*.

We of course still need to build our brands in the right way. However, if you do not focus as a business on making things as easy as possible for your consumers, or much more accurately your shoppers, to buy then you really do not have much hope. There needs to be a conscious rebalancing of Consumer and Shopper Marketing in your business ethos.

Why did Dollar Shave Club take off? Absolutely they had a great shareable video, but this had ease of purchase experience at its core. This was motivating enough for many shavers to trial the product, and they have not looked back since. In categories ripe for digital disruption such as shaving, D2C has taken off because it has fundamentally unlocked and responded to key shopper 'Triggers and Barriers'. These specific Triggers and Barriers have been exacerbated and enabled by the Digital Revolution in our industry.

This means that Shopper Marketing should become a dominant philosophy in your business. As a nice aside this may also help bring in those Light Buyers and penetration points so advocated as necessary by Byron Sharp in his clever book.

---

[20] Sharp, *How brands grow*.

All of this also lends weight to my point about thinking of 'd-Commerce' rather than 'e-Commerce'. This is not just about the sales and Purchase Journeys completed on retailer websites, it is about the whole essence of Omnichannel Shopper Marketing that supports and leads shoppers through a range of O2O (Online To Offline or vice versa) experiences. If *you* lead the shoppers through their Purchase Journeys, they will select *your* products ahead of your competitors'.

Shopper Marketing is all about influencing shoppers at the point of purchase decision along the P2P. With rapidly evolving (disappearing) notions of brand loyalty, this is more important than ever for the future health of your company.

Pictorially, we can also make the same point in this way:

Figure 3: Interaction of business functions.

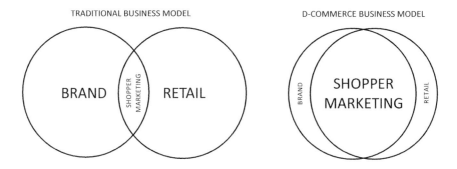

In the traditional CPG view of the world, the two great business leviathans of 'Brand' and 'Retail' rub against each other, and overlap in what we call 'Shopper Marketing'.

What has happened in the last ten or so years, is that the area of overlap between Brand and Retail has almost become much more marked, and we can look to D2C for a really good example of where this has happened in its entirety. There is only one thing that has really been the catalyst of this change, and this is the growth of d-Commerce in its widest context as described above.

For your business, this means that it is time to fully equip your Shopper team with the resources it needs to take the high ground (both internally and externally) in this space. Your brand marketers still have the key role to play as builders and facilitators of the brand, but what this means must evolve. If your company is not winning at the PoP both on and offline, then it will not be winning anything for much longer.

I recently read a great piece regarding P&G and Amazon in the US[21]. With absolute focus on the online PoP, the Tide Brand Managers designed packaging that was first and foremost created to maximise sales potential from the online shelf. Although the likes of P&G may move at bigger business pace towards a more shopper-centric approach, your business does not have to.

How many marketers in your business are still not yet fully supportive of the crucial importance of getting the Digital Packaging right for today's omnichannel shopper? Spending a bit of time and money there may bring much more incremental commercial benefit to your company than potentially wasting cash developing yet more cannibalising line extensions.

The kind of illusory Consumer Marketing that perpetuates legacy views of engagement should also have nowhere to hide in your business. The time for Shopper Marketing to shine is now.

Data in focus #3: Getting dirty with analytics and dashboarding.

In order to maximise the potential of d-Commerce in your business, you need to spend some time getting dirty with data. Good news is that it does not have to be onerous or require any amount of significant investment to make a solid start.

There is a lot of discussion around different kinds of data in business, and if you talk to people in other verticals, they often cite the 'lack of

---

[21] About Amazon. "Reinventing an American Icon"; https://blog.aboutamazon.com/sustainability/reinventing-an-american-icon (accessed March 20, 2019).

data' as a major barrier against CPG making the most of the latent digital potential in our industry. I cannot speak for your business, but I certainly have never experienced the feeling that any business I worked in is lacking data in any way!

What these outsiders mean, I think, is that they do not believe that we have the right *kind* of data in CPG, and specifically first party data. This is the kind of data that allegedly allows for deep, meaningful relationships with our shoppers. The data is proprietary, and typically may constitute some kind of CRM (Customer Relationship Management) fuelled database. But is having this kind of data a Healthy Distraction right now? Personally, I do not believe that it is for many businesses.

If you really wanted to establish a CRM database, then this is not, technically at least, a difficult thing to do. There are plenty of third-party solutions such as MailChimp available which will do more than a good enough job to get you started, so box ticked.

The question that I believe you should be asking yourself with regard to data, is what do you want data to *do* for your company? Here is another real-world example of where you need to be wary of the BNCs and whizzy solution vendors who have got their eyes firmly on your margin.

A couple of years ago, the must have marketing gizmo was some kind of Data Management Platform or DMP. Marketers and businesses were convinced that the solution to their marketing ills, lay not in being honest about the changing nature of consumer v shopper as discussed above, but in spending a small fortune on something that would work wonders with the real 21st century marketing currency of data. The DMP would somehow smash different datasets together and output gold dust insight that would help you win.

Quite a few businesses spent a small fortune on DMPs, and then within about six months stopped using them, or never even started. The reason for this will be explained in the section on Data Strategy in Chapter 5. For now, let us acknowledge a couple of much more pragmatic data truths:

1) Data has been around in CPG for quite some time.

2) Data can do many different things in businesses.

DMPs and similar initialisms are nothing but Unhealthy Distractions for most businesses. Most CPGs subscribe to one or two of the big data houses (eg Nielsen, Kantar, IRI) and buy data to understand business performance. There is a necessary corporate need for this and it should continue. But is your Return On Data Investment (RODI) as good as it could be?

How visible are your key online metrics in your business? Kantar World Panel, for example, gives a really useful read of share and sales in online and offline. Depending on the size of your business (ie its concurrent read in the panel), I would strongly endorse creating a simple online dashboard using Kantar data to help elucidate the online hits and misses.

More widely than that, why not also roll in some of your key social metrics or web performance highlights if relevant? Anyone can access the publicly available engagement numbers on Facebook, for example. Large numbers of fans are great, especially if they are of the human kind. But how many (what percentage) are engaging with your posts by liking them, commenting etc? This is a really helpful metric you can easily compare to your competitors', whilst also highlighting what your audience likes at the same time.

If you do have a CRM programme, then what is the open rate on your emails? Over 20% is good, and as another tip, look carefully at the subject line of your email message because that is the single biggest determinant of open rate. Test and Learn a bit!

If you are that way inclined, then dig a bit deeper using Google Analytics or Facebook Analytics; it is not nearly as scary as it sounds. There really is plenty you can do to unlock better RODI without heavyweight technology.

The key related point here is that you might not need to invest in new data sources, or third parties, to get a good feel for how you are performing online. There might not be an 'official' industry standard but that really is ok. A pragmatic approach towards understanding online performance is a really Healthy Distraction that it is easy to foster in any business.

Remember a key part of what we must do as d-Commerce evangelists is to be accountable, and part of this is owning and sharing the news of what is happening online with the wider business. Spend half a Box 2 day constructing a dashboard in PowerPoint, and a couple of hours a month updating it and sharing it with your colleagues. This will do wonders for the d-Commerce profile and wider business focus chez-vous.

Which brings us nicely to the question of ROI in its broader sense.

Every business needs to understand ROI better. I used to get quite frustrated by the trite request to 'prove' that digital works, often unaccompanied by a need to demonstrate similar rigour for more legacy methods. But no longer. What we need to develop is a way of understanding the impact of *all* of our investments, not an uncertain perspective on one that drives preference over another.

'Digital' in an unprovable regard should only really relate to the very murky Wild West corner of d-Marketing. The lack of transparency and potential for automated fraud makes it very difficult to 'prove' much there at all.

Amazon earnestly started its assault on the Facebook / Google d-Marketing budget duopoly in 2018. Since then it has been kicking out some interesting stats on the impact of advertising on its platform, and many brands are starting to reflect on their approach as a result. This supports the argument for a wider d-Commerce P2P media play in my view.

I think it is also increasingly difficult to 'prove' that big brand broadcast works. There is an argument to say that one reason why 'TV works' now is because it is a JBP lubricant for securing the best in store feature. It is the feature in store that 'works' and not the TV per se, especially in light of rapidly changing media consumption habits.

It could therefore be a good time to think about investing more of your marketing budget in a nicely joined up shopper-focused P2P campaign. You might save a few quid and also find that the door opens even more widely to some juicy in store feature.

So expect the ROI question to come up at some point on your d-Commerce journey. When it does, it may be beneficial to address it in the following terms. There are different things you can do to help demonstrate the ROI of your d-Commerce investment:

1) Do the basics well. By this I mean compile a database of activity and impact: what you did and what it drove against any relevant metrics. As part of this record what was actually implemented (screen grab) and keep it up to date. It is amazing how many businesses do not even do this, and I hope yours is not one of them.

2) Bring a bit of data science into your overall approach. Think about which Shopper Measure you are trying to drive (ie Frequency, Penetration, or Weight of Purchase), then design and implement your d-Commerce shopper plan and budget in the best way to deliver that objective. If you can get some impact data that will show after the investment whether the shopper objective was delivered or not, then get it.

3) If you do not have granularity of data to go down this route, then bring in science in another way. When I was at Pukka, I produced a simple one-page summary that compared all the online retailers by what 'soft payback' was returned for investment in terms of insight, cost, reach and targeting.

   This 'quick and dirty' ready-reckoner was very helpful to inform investment decisions. Much larger organisations have benefitted from versions of the same idea since.

4) Engage the retailer in the right way at the start of the investment

journey. Agree the need to have assessment data out at the other end, and this will face right into your ability and desire to better show ROI.

5) Do planning really well. Give absolute clarity to your business on what you want to do and why. This may also help your business understand that the multi-channel linear view of investment and return is not always valid. People do not shop in linear paths anymore, so investment in one channel may not just bring a return in that single channel.

A couple of these might be a bit more of a slow burn, but as a key part of a Digital Simplification programme, they can all have genuine value.

In conclusion, there is an awful lot you can do to champion the d-Commerce cause in your business by rolling up your sleeves and getting stuck in. Everything you try may not work, but I guarantee that at least some of it will.

Roll Your Sleeves Up in byte sized chunks.

- It is not just about the strategy.
- Do not expect to hide in a d-Commerce role.
- Do not assume that your online growth will just continue if you do not do anything about it.
- Learn what you can from SMEs.
- Shopper Marketing needs to be a leading marketing philosophy in your business.
- Data is accessible to all. It is not a new thing in your business and there is no need to be scared of it.
- Own communication of d-Commerce metrics in your business.
- There are many different ways to answer the ROI question. Start answering it in at least one way right now.

CHAPTER 4. BRING IN THE DIGITAL GUY?

Digital comes, digital goes.

ONE OF THE questions that gets asked a lot in d-Commerce (and d-Business) more widely, is what is the best Operating Model? Businesses want to know how their peers are serving the digital opportunity, what Best In Class (BIC) looks like, whether you should have a standalone business function or functional experts; that kind of thing.

Without knowing the intricacies of your own business, its ambitions and its state of evolution, it really is impractical to give a definitive 'do it like this' answer. What works or worked for a given business at a given time may not work for that same business at a different time, or even for your business at this current time at all.

What I would advocate as a start point is agreeing and providing clarity for exactly what you want your digital person or function to *do*. Once you have clarity in this area, then provide that person or team with full accountability to get on and do it for the reasons I have already laid out.

The kind of things that your d-Commerce person or team could do might include Account Management responsibility for some or all of the

Dotcom and Pure Play customers. Within this, carefully align limited resources with commercial opportunities because that is just sensible business planning. If you need to prioritise, then start with the Dotcoms first.

More widely, does your digital team or person also have responsibility for sub-functions such as d-Category or d-Shopper? This is where some of the 'low hanging fruit' will absolutely be found. If your d-Commerce person does not have the bandwidth to cover these sub-functions too, then your central Category or Shopper resource absolutely must.

After those two bases are covered, then it really is a question of the appetite and ability of your business to really unlock d-Commerce or not. Having some dedicated insight and finance resource would be great, but clearly at some point you need to reconcile the d-Commerce opportunity with other opportunities in your business.

In your overall Sales Channel Strategy where does d-Commerce sit in relation to Discounters or Convenience for example? Do you have a clear idea of the relative 'Size of the Prize' of unlocking these disparate sales channels versus a 'do nothing' scenario? I will return later to a methodology you could use to understand this. For now, I just want to spend a moment on Operating Model evolution.

As can be seen in the diagram below, there are broadly four different stages of evolution in the d-Commerce (or d-Business) Operating Model. Generally speaking this would be a sensible path to follow on the way to d-Maturity, but of course it may need to be adapted to suit your particular business circumstances.

Figure 5: Organisational evolution of d-Business resource.

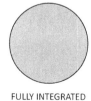

| ARBITRARY RESOURCE MODEL | CENTRE OF EXCELLENCE MODEL | HUB AND SPOKE MODEL | FULLY INTEGRATED MODEL |

The Arbitrary Resource Model is where most businesses start off at some point. There is no real Operating Model to speak of, and pockets of need are arbitrarily apportioned to different parts of the business driven by short term factors. This may include having a nominal Digital Guy, without full consideration having been applied to some of the prioritisation factors talked about above.

From the d-Business perspective there are minimal advantages to this approach, other than an attempt at BAU management of specific areas. The major drawbacks are a lack of coherent focus and strategy, and only ad hoc levels of capability across the function or wider business.

The next evolutionary stage may be something like a Centre of Excellence (CoE). This is where dedicated d-Commerce and d-Marketing 'specialist' resource sit together in one team, and are the go to folk for all digital questions and answers.

The advantages of this model are that it can be a fast-track to driving significant upskilling in Digital Capability across the business. Key roles can be selected and recruited for, and the CoE can have clear ownership of key project areas.

Because commercial functions such as Sales and Marketing are in the same place, it can, theoretically at least, be a useful conduit for knowledge sharing across the business. The lean and agile nature of the team should also mean that it is able to work quickly on targeted priorities. With regard to reporting line, because it contains experts from different functions then the team can sit comfortably in different parts of the overall business structure.

There are however some downsides to this Operating Model too. The team can be seen as separate from the business, struggle with alignment or even to be 'running away with it' when it comes to the digital plan. As I explained above, any successful Digital Simplification initiative needs to take the business with it, or the chances of long-term change are significantly diminished.

This risk of a siloed operating model may also mean longer term there is no business benefit at all, as there is very little integration of the capabilities back into the wider business functions. Over reliance on the CoE could leave the wider business exposed when key people or business priorities move on. The team members constituting the CoE, though doubtlessly experts in their field, may not have the wider skillset necessary to meaningfully integrate their work practices into the wider company.

The third stage Hub and Spoke can be a natural evolution of the CoE. This, like the CoE model, also involves a small team of Subject Matter Experts (SMEs[22]), but this time they sit in their respective functions rather than as a standalone unit. There is in effect a small central team of SMEs, but this time the resource is embedded in the corresponding business functions.

On the plus side, this can result in better integration of capability into the business. There can be a wider company benefit of increased sharing of digital learnings across all areas (no silos), and some potential economies of scale via digital product development happening in more than one place (eg customer or brand) at once.

The main watch outs of this model are the potential duplication of activities within spokes, and the potential for confusion around the spokes' true 'home'. This may also manifest itself as duplication externally, if for example there is potential for overlap in key customer contacts. Depending on the size, scale and complexity of your customers' businesses, it may or may not be a problem to have multiple points of contact in the supply side.

As was also the case with the CoE model, the Hub and Spoke is not best thought of as a long-term solution, as expertise will still be largely held by the SMEs in the team. Additionally, these positions may in some ways also be harder to recruit for, as expertise may be needed in both the digital subject area and in the embedding function.

---

[22] SME colloquially stands for both Small and Medium-sized Enterprise and Subject Matter Expert. SME only refers to the latter in Chapter 4.

The final stage of evolution, and one that many digital folk talk about as the end point where their digital roles will not actually exist anymore, is the Fully Integrated Model. Here d-Commerce and d-Marketing expertise is fully managed and embedded within each brand and customer team.

This ensures deep internal capability where it is needed, and can make it easier to manage customers and brands as the teams are in effect a single entity (ie no 'digital experts'). This should also create a more meaningful omnichannel experience for the consumers and shoppers, thereby creating a business that is fit for the future on multiple fronts.

Whereas this is a sensible desired state, the practicalities of delivering this can be resource heavy. It is likely to be time consuming to achieve, and, more likely than not, external resource will be needed to help navigate the necessary interfaces and skills gaps that could be blockers to its realisation in your business today.

As an absolute mandatory for this approach, the kind of cross business tailored support talked about in the section on Digital Capability above would need careful consideration to ensure a thorough hearts and minds job is achieved.

What works offline works online too.

Some of the things that will help on your d-Business organisational journey will already exist in your business today. As I have hopefully already gone some way to convincing you, if you can make the digital world appear less complex and intimidating, then it will only help your existing colleagues feel more comfortable as they happily tread the d-Path.

One thing that it may help to start asking as a matter of routine is 'what is the d-Commerce version of that?'. For example, you may already have a Channel Planning process in your business, so as part of this build the d-Commerce Channel Plan following the same methodology/ template completion as you are doing for your other channels (eg Grocery,

Convenience, Discounters, Wholesale, and Specialist if relevant).

What I would encourage you to do as well, is to try and break down your d-Commerce channel into the appropriate subchannels (possibly in the same way that you do for Convenience: Symbols, Independents, Multiple Convenience etc).

The relevant d-Commerce subchannels would be Dotcoms (or Bricks & Clicks if you prefer), Pure Play, B2B, D2C, Third Party and possibly Specialist. Third Party may include things like Quick Service Restaurants or specific apps; it depends mainly on the product category in which you operate.

Staying at the total d-Commerce channel level, spend some time thinking about subchannel prioritisation. If you have some comparative data to build an assessment on, then use this. If not then a Boston Matrix like the one below is a completely valid subchannel prioritisation tool for any part of your business. If your business size warrants it, you could also complete a customer overlay.

Figure 6: Customer or subchannel prioritisation tool.

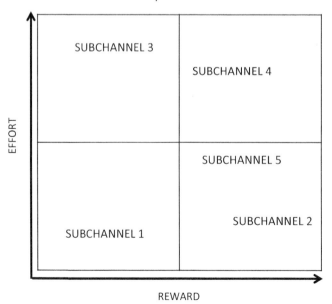

The idea is to start working on the subchannels where the effort to reward ratio is the most positive. Typically, this would be high reward for low effort. So, in the example above, your top priority would be subchannel 2 followed by subchannel 5. The low reward high effort subchannels should be addressed last if at all (subchannel 3 above), with the others falling in the middle.

If you do not have a data-based view to build into your prioritisation matrix today, then do not despair. 'Gut feel' can be as good a place as any to start (Test and Learn is okay here too!), although it is probably a good idea to apply a bit more science if you can.

To support your prioritisation planning, it could be worth working through a robust process for Channel Planning. The 'Bow Tie' illustration below works well for this at any channel or subchannel level.

Figure 7: d-Commerce Channel Plan derivation process.

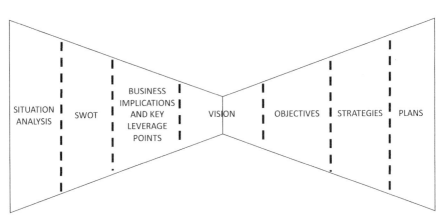

Starting with an insight trawl, the Situation Analysis is designed to help you thoroughly appraise the channel as it is today, whilst identifying relevant areas to think about for the future. This is then pulled into a summary SWOT, which is then crystallised further into Business Implications (built from Weaknesses and Threats) and Key Leverage Points (built from Strengths and Opportunities).

If you can, it is then worth simplifying this further into a one- or two-line Channel Vision. Then from this work through Objectives, Strategies, and finally, Plans.

Another O2O translate to think about is Perfect Store. Apply the exact same principles to building your Perfect Online Store to those that you apply to your offline version: best practice shelf layout, merchandising guidelines, Category Management etc; there is an online equivalent to all of these stalwarts of Perfect Store-dom. Have a Perfect Online Store that covers what Perfect Store means, how you execute it, how you measure implementation and what can be done to make improvements, and you will have a great practical tool for your Sales team.

We can continue the O2O theme: what does great shopper service (engagement) look like online? d-Businesses like Amazon make no bones whatsoever of their 'Customer {Shopper} Obsession'. Just as you probably have an idea of what is great from the shopper perspective for your offline stores (eg information at the PoP, investment in appropriate store media), then again be very clear on what the d-Commerce equivalent of this is too.

Your products' online PoP is *the* gateway to shopper engagement and satisfaction online. Ensure it works just as hard as your offline gateway and your shoppers will thank you for it (sometimes even with a nice shareable review!).

To help here, it may be useful to define and embed in your business thinking some of the key Triggers and Barriers to shopping online. People shop online for reasons such as convenience, bargain hunting, availability, privacy, budget control. The key Barriers are things like fulfilment delay (ie you do not get your product immediately), lack of sensory stimulation (smell, feel), delivery cost, social limitations.

In addition to these channel considerations, there will of course be further Triggers and Barriers specific to your category; the above is not intended to be an exhaustive list. Do not forget that we are all shoppers who just want to shop, and so principles that your business can apply to influence purchase decisions in an offline store have parallels in the online world too.

This is probably as a good a juncture as any to reinforce the principle of introducing an omnichannel view of the shopper into your business. Granted this may be an area where some external pointers in the right direction are required, but it really is a mandatory for d-Commerce glory.

'Omnichannel' in essence refers to how people shop nowadays. People no longer shop in a linear fashion: ie a Purchase Journey does not start and end in a single sales channel as it used to do before the advent of online shopping. Although the Purchase Journey will still be fulfilled in a single channel (eg on a Dotcom site, in a big store), all the considerations and influences that occur en route will come from a mixture of online and offline sources.

Fortunately we can still plan against this, as will be covered in more detail in the section on Omnichannel Playbooks in Chapter 5. For now, it will suffice to give clarity to what we mean when we talk about a Purchase Journey and why this is important.

'Purchase Journey' is a universal principle that can be applied to any omnichannel shopper journey, whether it is majority online, majority offline or more equal amounts of both. As Shopper Marketers we have the opportunity to influence shoppers' purchase decisions at each stage of the Purchase Journey, and our ability to do this is helped by knowledge of which Triggers and Barriers are particularly relevant at each stage.

All shoppers go through a Purchase Journey on the way to making a product selection. This has been accepted knowledge in the offline world for some time, and it is just as valid for online, or omnichannel, too. Chances are that there is already a view of Purchase Journey in your business. It may well be expressed as a P2P which includes:

1) Consider: ie influence the shopper's choice at the first moment of product consideration with the aim of getting on the shopping list.

2) Engage: ie when the shopper has started the shopping journey, influence their choices before they buy.

3) Buy: ie at the point of product selection, ensure that it is your product that goes into the basket.

4) Repeat: ie keep the shopper engagement going after the purchase is completed so they come back and buy again.

These Purchase Journey, Perfect Store and Channel Planning principles can all be translated from their offline equivalents to online. If you do this then it might not be such a challenging leap to become a d-Commerce ninja as you may think.

What is my online Size of the Prize?

Omnichannel P2P planning and execution is absolutely the gateway through which to pass if your business is serious about winning today's shopper. What may also help your business along the way, is an opportunity evaluation which is more aligned to the way that the business wheels currently turn.

As an industry I do not believe we are that close yet to being able to credibly work out the scalable value of an omnichannel Purchase Journey, or series of journeys. This would involve some very intricate modelling of the specific contribution of various on and offline influencing factors on the eventual single channel destination for spend.

I know that some CPG businesses are already conducting specific omnichannel journey research, and this has resulted in some interesting analyses of the value of very specific journey types. I am not yet aware of a scalable O2O attribution model that could really paint the opportunity size of omnichannel in totality. But we can take some baby steps.

As I explained above, most CPG businesses, for understandable reasons, are still oriented around the multi-channel model. There are Grocery sales teams, Convenience teams, Discounter teams and depending on the state of organisational evolution along the d-Commerce path, most likely a Digital Guy or two as well.

Customers need servicing, P&L accountability needs to ensured; so a multi-channel approach to the Sales function is the right one today. This does not preclude an omnichannel shopper philosophy of course.

In this vein, it is well worth making some effort to work out the size of the online channel sales opportunity in your business. If you do subscribe to the notion that a significant proportion of your offline sales are influenced by online as well, and of course I heartily encourage you to do so, then the online channel opportunity you evaluate may even be under-calling the prize. The commercial benefit of winning d-Commerce will likely be higher than the linear online channel opportunity you work out.

Opportunity sizing, like many of the O2O principles laid out above, is of course not new in businesses. Of course, it is possible to invest significant money in econometric modelling, cannibalisation studies, pricing elasticity and so forth. At the right time in your business this may represent money well spent. But do we need to go down this highly sophisticated route to get a credible opportunity size for online? I do not believe that we do.

The methodology for opportunity sizing that I have deployed on numerous occasions follows the same basic three-step process. This has been used with comprehensive Panel and EPOS data combined, with Panel data only, with a mixture of desk research and EPOS, and even once in Africa for CV opportunity sizing where in all honesty we had to make half of it up.

You of course need to make the exercise as rigorous as you can, and its robustness will be largely determined by the depth and breadth of data available. It is essential that you record the assumptions you make behind growth rates or proxy data sources, and you should expect to spend a sensible amount of time explaining your methodology to your colleagues.

You should also expect to deploy some Level 2 Excel skills (where Level 1 is adding borders and shading), and of course a familiarity with the data sources you are using will help too.

The basic three-step opportunity sizing process is: establish a baseline; model alternative growth scenarios; model alternative share scenarios. That is it, three simple steps.

Your baseline should ideally be worked out at total channel or category level. This will simultaneously enable you to apply total channel or category growth trends to it in step one, whilst also sensibly evaluating your business's Size of the Prize via share modelling in step three. Your baseline can be intricately built up at subcategory, subchannel or customer level, or you could just use a credible source located via your favourite search engine.

Once you have established your baseline, you need to look back at history (two years minimum ideally but can be done with one), and then project forwards different scenarios: does growth / decline continue at the same rate; does it drop off or increase. Again, be crystal clear on the assumptions that you make, discuss with others, and amend through consensus.

Finally overlay your target share. What can work well here is a 'do nothing' scenario where you lose share because you, well, do nothing and your competitors do something; a 'maintain' scenario where your current trajectory is maintained; and a 'growth' scenario where you manage to pull your fingers out of your ears and use your hands to grab hold of a commercial prize instead. I normally then express the opportunity value over a three-year time frame as the difference between 'growth' and 'do nothing'.

Now of course within here there are a number of levels of sophistication and variables that can be considered. It would be prudent to plan for a fair investment of time to work through inception, data sourcing, modelling and alignment for whichever level you may choose to go to.

Some businesses work out Size of the Prize using share alone (ie over/under trade) without either of the first two steps. I do not personally think this is robust enough if the output is going to be used to justify major resourcing decisions. You should not overcomplicate things, but be careful not to oversimplify either.

A more detailed walk through of the methodology recently deployed to work out a Dotcom and Pure Play opportunity size went like this:

1) Online category baseline established using Panel data over the last two years.

2) Total company share baseline established by overlaying company performance onto the above.

3) Customer and subcategory performance broken down as far as the data allowed and steps 1 and 2 repeated at that level.

4) Key Shopper Measures (Penetration, Frequency, Weight of Purchase) added in at customer level.

5) Amazon data added at supplier or category level (you too will be able to do this if they were kind enough to agree to hand it over *before* you signed the cheque).

6) Excel Level 1 shading and border formatting applied.

7) Finance asked nicely to translate the Panel RSV into internal revenue.

8) Shopper Measures added at step 4 tweaked to model what will happen at customer level over the next three years.

9) Big dollop of common sense applied.

10) Customer share targets overlaid to work it all through into a nice customer bridge and a three-year opportunity.

As long as you carefully record and explain your assumptions, and invest the required time in alignment, alignment, alignment, then there is no reason at all why this opportunity size cannot become the de facto number for your business to use for planning purposes.

Although Panel data does overstate branded share, and is not EPOS, it is still fine to use in this exercise. Actually, in the example above I even sense checked the Panel numbers versus EPOS in a couple of customers where we had the data depth to do this. Once you ensure that the Panel and EPOS providers are reading the category by the same definition, then the corresponding sales value numbers really are very close.

Other general points would be, that because you work out the baseline based on current subchannel or category trajectory, then the incremental number is more like a true incremental number (ie current growth rates are stripped out). You could make further assumptions for sale steal versus in store, but I personally believe that because your opportunity is worked out at share level, then you are effectively talking about nicking your competitors' online sales rather than your own in store ones anyhow.

The final thing, which is really neat, is that because your opportunity has been worked out at Shopper Measure level, then you now know *exactly* which levers to pull to make your dreams come true. We will come back to this point in Chapter 5.

If you do not have/ cannot get this depth of data, then that is not necessarily a problem. Follow the same basic three-step approach and you will get as good a Size of the Prize number as you can.

Different markets, same solutions.

During my time spent as a freelance consultant, I was fortunate enough to work with a range of businesses across CPG categories and markets. Although the nuances of each business and market were different as you might expect, when it came to d-Commerce there was, and still is, a significant amount of common ground in the questions that the businesses are trying to answer.

The big strategic ones are in areas such as resourcing, opportunity size, integration; that kind of thing. One of the most common questions of all though is simply 'What should we *do*?'. How do we make sense of all this potential d-Commerce execution and cut through to what is important?

Get ready for the re-entry of The 5 Ps and a couple of years spent touring European markets delivering d-Commerce training for a major global brand.

Through a contact (never underestimate the power of who you know!), I was asked to help build and deliver an e-Commerce and Digital Shopper Marketing (aka d-Commerce) workshop-based training programme. The programme was to be centrally sponsored and rolled out across multiple markets and commercial functions.

The brief was to design a programme that would inspire the workshop attendees to champion d-Commerce back into their business; to simplify the complex; to give clear pointers on what to do and how to win; to increase their knowledge levels: all that good stuff.

At the appropriate moment in the creation and sign off journey, I nervously put forward 'something I had done before' as a potential inclusion that may deliver some of the training objectives. Following some understandable pressure testing and clarification, The 5 P Framework was taken forwards as something being worthy of consideration.

As was also the case previously, the actual definition of each P changed slightly from what had been used before. This is absolutely fine, and actually helps if some of the other people involved have some ownership too. Again, it was the simple galvanising effect of complete prioritisation via The 5 P approach that resonated the most.

For sure the eventual workshops also included some other great d-Commerce stuff, but it was consistently the case that The 5 Ps featured positively and prominently in the post workshop feedback.

This particular iteration of The 5 Ps was as follows:

1) Pure and Simple. This is pretty much exactly what it says on the tin:

make sure everything you do is as straightforward as possible, and if it is on brand then even better.

Amazon 'One Click to Buy' is good example of Pure and Simple, as are other user-focused-shopper-friendly actions. If you can make the purchase experience as easy as possible when someone is shopping online, then quite frankly they are more likely to buy something (remember 'ease of shop' is both one of the key online channel triggers that we talked about above, and an absolute mandatory in CPG today).

A good way of seeing Pure and Simple brought to life is on Dotcom, where the most successful executions are often the most straightforward ones. This is especially true when shopping from a mobile, as the small screen size has to work as efficiently as possible.

2) Personalised Connections. As with all other iterations, personalisation and the power of data featured prominently in these Ps as well. There is an increasing expectancy amongst shoppers to have a personalised experience when they shop, and if you can tap into shoppers' latent desire for this online, then you can make more meaningful connections with them (= sell more) too.

With the advent of 5G and the exponential increase of data available, we need to find a way to make this accessible without getting scared. In 2010 Eric Schmidt talked about how we create as much information every 2 days as we did up to 2003[23]. Now people are thinking about when the amount of available data will start doubling every twelve hours[24].

3) Perfect Content. As we have already highlighted, the online world thrives on content. If you can make the Content that you own,

---

[23] Tech Crunch. "Eric Schmidt: Every 2 Days We Create As Much Information As We Did Up To 2003"; https://techcrunch.com/2010/08/04/schmidt-data/ (accessed March 20, 2019).
[24] Digital Journal. "Op-Ed: Knowledge doubles almost every day, and it's set to increase"; http://www.digitaljournal.com/tech-and-science/science/op-ed-knowledge-doubles-almost-every-day-and-it-s-set-to-increase/article/537543 (accessed March 20, 2019).

curate or create as Perfect as possible, then your shoppers are more likely to engage with it, talk about it, and use it in their lives.

Included in here would be all the relevant Fix the Basics elements, BIC parts of your Perfect Store, online Category Management principles and more.

4) Pioneering Solutions. Similar to part of the essence of Partner of Choice, this is where you think about your willingness to try new stuff, either on your own or in partnership with key customers. This is as much a state of mind as it is a way of doing business. Do not forget that as part of this you have to accept that sometimes the things you try might not work.

5) Present Where Relevant. Rather than being present everywhere, to make the most meaningful connections with your busy shoppers you may have to make sure the connections are relevant for who they are, where they are, and what they are doing at a given time. If you can do this successfully then your business may have a much more meaningful and beneficial relationship with its shoppers.

This is all about being there at the time your shoppers either want, or might want, to interact with you: fitting your solutions around them. You need to be aware of what your shoppers need from brands at key moments of the Purchase Journey, and then find the best ways to deliver solutions to them. In other words, make full use of Triggers and Barriers.

It is very clear that many different businesses need similar things, although often at different stages of their d-Commerce journey. Everyone passes through the same opportunity articulation-knowledge seeking-learning path, just maybe at different times and rates.

We all need to have a 'never stop learning and improving' kaizen mentality to win in d-Commerce, and this has been my exact experience with lovely data too.

Data in focus #4: My Eureka moment.

As you may have gathered, my personal journey down the data-brick road has not been an entirely positive experience. A couple of unsure steps forward, one step back, hide behind a desk, come out confidently smiling whilst inwardly dying. That sort of thing.

The idea of 'data' for some equates only to rows and rows of too small font size detail, tables stuffed in the appendices of killer decks, and esoteric Excel formulas worthy of GCHQ level encryption practice. Not necessarily what might get you up in the morning full of the joys of spring.

This was also my initial view of data. Nowadays, I actually quite like data, and in the spirit of winning the d-Commerce long game, data is something that we all need to start liking too.

My own personal Eureka moment came when I was running a workshop with a room full of IT, Commercial and Legal people. It was not quite an Archimedean lower myself into a bathtub experience, but my co-facilitator did look a bit like Archimedes at least.

The workshop was about mapping different data entities together, and working through some use cases to really start thinking through how data could come to life. On the surface this may not seem like the stuff of paradigm shifts, but it was all very Agile, and suddenly something went click. From that moment on, the business changing power of what properly managed and applied data can deliver to the bottom line became a big part of my life. Really!

If you are already a big data-phile, then there is no need for you to reappraise your perception of data in business. If you are more of a data-phobe, then it might be worth trying some new stuff with your business data like I did.

At the same time, you might also find that you start to generate much better RODI from the data that is already in your business and the stuff you buy on an ad hoc basis to boot. You will also be more likely to ensure that the data you buy in the future is what you actually need. Data needs to be so much more in your business than the fuel of business reporting. To elevate data to a more deserving status, here are a few things to think about:

1) Be crystal clear on the question that you want your data to answer.

   Now I am sure we all do this all the time already, but just in case not everyone in your business agrees with you, then spend a bit of time forging that clarity, pressure testing it, checking it again, and then bouncing it off a child.

   If you cannot simply articulate the issue/ problem statement that you want your data to answer, read the above paragraph again. And again. Then make your problem statement shorter. When you have this clarity:

2) Be rigorous and honest with your existing resources' ability to answer the question.

   Most businesses these days have a fairly substantial library of qual and quant data from which they build strategy, look for opportunities, explain performance and so forth.

   Can your existing data pool adequately answer the challenge you have set yourself? Can your people process the data well enough to find the answer your business seeks? Are the killer insights easily accessible and known by all those that could use them?

   If that was 'Three Yeses' (or should it be Four, I do not really watch the X Factor) then move on to point 5. If not:

3) Ask a Digital Guy for help (or maybe even just for a fresh pair of eyes).

   There is *a lot* of data out there. By asking an impartial Digital Guy who has no vested interest in selling you more of it, some chinks of light may start to shine through.

4) Bring the tools into your business that will address Data Capability in the right way.

A lot of money has been wasted in CPG via buying tech that businesses neither need nor are ready for. Every pound squandered on these outlays is a pound less to be spent on some really cool Omnichannel Shopper Marketing. Make sure your business spending is in those areas that *will* make a difference, and if it is using or doing something that is not helping then just be honest and let it go. Test and Learn is okay.

Technology should always be business enabling. Ensure that the tech you buy into is not business disabling instead.

5) Make understanding ROI a cornerstone of your approach to data and insight.

Data is a key part of any sensible approach to ROI such as those discussed in Chapter 3. Remember that it is not necessary to have all the answers to start taking ROI more seriously, although you will probably need a bit of data at some point.

Taking ROI seriously is a great way to make data science sing in your business. If you start to get a feel for what really is working or not working for you, then you may even have one or two Eureka moments yourself.

Bring In The Digital Guy? in byte sized chunks.

- See your d-Commerce journey as an evolution of required resources. The Operating Model you end up with will be different from the one when you started.
- Replicate your offline approach onto online if you are unsure where to begin.
- Shoppers do not actively differentiate between online and offline channels. Engage and satisfy them whenever they interact with your products.

- Break the d-Commerce channel down into subchannels and work out what you want to achieve at subchannel level.
- Follow the three-step approach to work out Size of the Prize.
- Different markets and different businesses are looking for the same answers. 5 Ps traverse borders.
- Work out what you want data to do in your business and plug any associated capability gaps.
- Ensure your tech is business enabling and not business disabling.
- Expect data to bring Eureka moments into your life.

CHAPTER 5. D-COMMERCE DECODED

When the BNCs go home.

I F YOU WANT to succeed in d-Commerce, then as we have already said you absolutely need to have a kaizen mindset. Bring this learning philosophy into your business through the power of role-modelling and you will be taking some good solid steps.

Businesses may need to learn on a number of levels to deliver what is best for them, and I have already touched on some of the organisational capability challenges that you may encounter along the way.

This organisational capability may be required across different areas: employees, IT systems, policies, processes and so forth. As a result of this some businesses start off by calling in the BNCs to benchmark and deliver a helicopter view. Cue the DT 'opportunity' that your business may or may not need.

I personally do not believe that you need to bring in the BNCs to highlight a digital or d-Commerce opportunity in your business, although I am aware that many do go down this route.

Once the BNCs have delivered their last sermon and collected their final paycheck (possibly through slightly consultant-creep-failure gritted teeth), there is a chance that you might be left with a slight sense of flux.

What you have possibly also been left with, is your version of some standard BNC charts and spreadsheets. Whilst these will doubtlessly highlight your d-Commerce or digital opportunity, they may also provide slightly less clarity than required on how to turn all of that great content into a workable operational plan.

Having this operational plan gap between the high-level strategy and the day to day is not an uncommon thing to have in CPG. Neither is it uncommon for the C-Suite sponsored and endorsed digital plan to not be immediately deliverable, for a host of very valid reasons, by the Digital Guy.

Whether you started your d-Commerce journey with or without the BNC groundworks, the first thing you will likely do is Fix the Basics. Quick basics fixing checklist in case you were asleep when we covered this earlier:

1) Product images sorted. Marketing colleagues successfully cajoled into owning Digital Packaging in the same way that they own the physical stuff. As a result, multiple high-quality images with different pack angles and configurations are up to date and handily loaded into Brandbank, and Amazon dealt with too.

2) Some delicious Hero flavoured icing slathered on top. Marketing colleagues accepting of the fact that a 1cm image of the same pack that sits loud and proud on the supermarket shelves, might not have the best chance of being selected for the digital basket when the same shopper is scrolling frantically through their mobile screen. Consequently, you now also have mobile ready images with brand, variant, product count or other key usage information very clearly called out.

3) Nomenclature is accurate and shopper friendly. Can be pulled from New Line Forms so that could be a good place to start harmonising.

Once the basics are on the way to being sorted, it is a good time to think about a few more things:

1) A robust and sensible audit plan: measure; manage; optimise. There are a number of impressive looking third-party solutions you can buy into here, or alternatively you can save the cash and do it yourself. There is a suggested methodology to follow in the very next section.

   Quick point to note on third-party automated audit solutions: when they give a website a green light from the operational perspective, this may just mean that the site is working ok from the technical point of view. This does not necessarily mean that it is working for the online shopper. Artificial Intelligence has not yet reached this level of human endeavour in d-Commerce in my awareness; some human eyes with proper shopper knowledge behind them may colour code a web presence differently.

2) A search strategy aligned within the business, and ideally owned by your marketing colleagues. What are the category, brand, and product-associated search terms we want our products to come back against, when a shopper enters the term in the 'search' box on the retailer site? Some of your retailer partners will have solutions like a 'Search Term Optimiser' that will give insight-based lists of terms that shoppers usually associate with your products (likely available to you in return for some Bitcoin or other digital investment).

   Quick point on retailer search algorithms: no one except some people in the retailer know exactly how they work. Whereas things have definitely moved on in Pure Play and Dotcom from alphabetised lists, they have not yet on some B2B sites. For the Pure Plays and Dotcoms things like sales volume, product reviews, supplier cash, content quality, promotions and number of returns will all influence the search result position to some extent.

3) A robust understanding of what media options are available in your retailer, how much they cost, and what they will do.

Quick point on retailer media options: create an Omnichannel Shopper Playbook. Keep reading.

If you can tick off all three things from both lists, then you are definitely out of the d-Commerce blocks. To keep running in a straight line, it is quite possible that your business may not be entirely clear on what to do next.

Consequently, I have found it helpful to develop a structured sequence of stages that your business may wish to move through to win. This model may therefore provide your business with a solid operational roadmap.

Developing maturity.

As I have already explained, different businesses or markets are at different stages of the d-Commerce evolutionary journey. Each has wrestled with the same questions and some have even found the same answers.

Because each business or market is passing, or has passed, through the same stages along the way, I have developed a simple Maturity Model to lay out these stages in an accessible manner. All businesses will move through the five stages at some point, and chances are that your business has already tried some things at one or more levels.

To give yourselves the best chance of winning, however, I strongly recommend that you move through the stages in order. Also, complete each one thoroughly as they are all important.

Figure 8: d-Commerce Maturity Model.

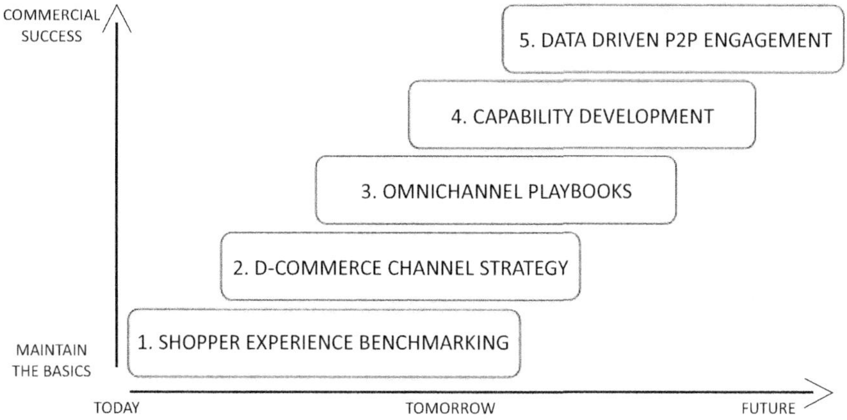

The first stage is to complete a thorough assessment of the SX of your brands online. This will give you a very clear understanding of where you are today, most likely highlight some Fix the Basics type quick wins, and provide a good ready reckoner to feed back into your business of how you are showing up online.

There are some nicely packaged, visually pleasing off the peg solutions available that can help here. Depending on your business budget and culture this may be what works best for you. Personally, I think your fledgling d-Commerce budget can be better spent in other areas like influencing shoppers but it really is your call.

If you do go down the off the peg route, then you need to ensure that all appropriate areas are properly investigated. The kinds of areas that you want covering include things like search performance, a content check (images, words), assortment (products on sale and how they interact), transition or navigation through retailer sites, plus a good look at reviews. Only by checking all these areas will you get a balanced picture of the SX for your brands.

These are very much things that you can check for yourself via some desk research (it is an SX review after all!). If uncertainty or time pressures make this option unviable, then such an assessment can easily be outsourced and shared back with your business with screen grabs, prioritised lists, quick fixes etc in good old PowerPoint.

When you have a good understanding of the SX, it is time to move on to your d-Commerce Channel Strategy. As already covered there are a few things that it would be good to include here: a Situation Analysis; Size of the Prize; a P or 4 or 5; maybe a trade story. Either complete this at total channel level or break it down to subchannel. Because you completed the SX review first, this will make your channel strategy much more meaningful.

Depending on your business needs, as with any strategy this could be fairly light touch or much more in depth. The customer or wider business requirements on the back of the strategy may largely determine what you include. Your strategy could be built out to cover a full eJBP approach, for example, or other things like a projection of the resourcing requirements in the medium term. You may want to include Perfect Online Store here too.

The next stage is to create an Omnichannel Playbook. A decent playbook will give your business complete clarity on where to play, and how to win the omnichannel shopper from the point of view of the different shopper media solutions (tools) available to your business. These will largely comprise the suite of investment options provided by your retail partners, although if done thoroughly your playbook could also include some non-retail native tools as well (eg Buy It Now from digital media or a third-party app).

What is of crucial significance here, is that your playbook should include both traditional and digital tools. From the shoppers' perspective, no differentiation whatsoever is made between something that may influence them online or offline. Apart from possibly when it concerns the staunchest of digital dinosaurs, most shoppers are influenced by both digital and traditional tools at some point (hence omnichannel).

Unless everyone in your business already has complete understanding of how to influence the omnichannel shopper, and you have produced a visually impactful, interactive playbook that gives complete clarity with new-iPhone-box-opening-smoothness to the following factors, then create an Omnichannel Playbook before going any further.

Your playbook should include clear guidance on:

- Which traditional and digital Shopper Marketing tools to use precisely at which stage of the Purchase Journey.
- How these tools may vary by product category if this is relevant in your business.
- What the priority of each tool is.
- Which Shopper Measures the tools deliver against.
- How the tools compare on key metrics like Reach, Engagement, Cost and ROI.
- Which Triggers and Barriers the tools help overcome.
- What is their relevance to specific shopper missions.

These last two may not be necessary depending on how shopper savvy your business is already.

Providing this level of granularity and focus in your business is crucial. It will simultaneously give guidance across the business in terms of what to do and why, whilst making your business feel comfortable that it knows what it is doing and how to make sound business decisions.

It will also very nicely tick the d-Commerce Shiny Things box, and is in my view a much better investment of limited resources than some of the other options already mentioned in this chapter.

When these first three stages are complete, then it is a good time to think about Capability Development. I am often asked why this is not lower down in the Maturity Model, and the answer is twofold.

First of all, I believe there is much you can do in your business to start making very solid d-Commerce progress before reaching for the Learning and Development chequebook. In the same vein, the output of your work on Levels 1 through 3 can also find a very useful home in the capability environment: ie let us educate ourselves on how we are currently showing up online, what our strategic approach is, and how we are going to make investment decisions. You may find that there are some noticeable omissions from the training deck if you do not have these things covered first.

The second reason for Capability Development being at Level 4 on the Maturity Model, is that as already explained, what capability means in your business may be quite different to what it means elsewhere. Your unique learning culture and wider capability needs for d-Commerce will likely only become apparent as you work through the first three stages.

It could well be the case, for example, that a tiered or blended solution is needed. It is likely that your business will have employees with the need for a range of d-Commerce skills and knowledge. Whereas all could possibly benefit from raising the digital bar, it may be more sensible to really target d-Commerce skills enhancement at a smaller group. Consequently, it may make sense for your business to have some kind of Foundation, Intermediate and Advanced capability programme, but this may not be the required solution for all.

Another consideration to bear in mind, is that your preferred methodology for training solution delivery will likely be an extension of your wider corporate approach. If your business is the type that encourages collaboration, wants its employees to learn through doing, and sees the formal training environment as only part of the skills growth journey, then you would be wise to follow 70:20:10 principles. This means 70% of learning occurs on the job, 20% is done via mentoring/ Line Manager support and only 10% is formally trained.

Other businesses may be better suited to e-Learning or 'skill pill' type solutions where targeted punchy modules are developed and delivered, often at scale, through digital means. It all really does depend on having worked out what is right for you. Spend some time working through the foundation levels of the model before thinking about capability more widely.

The final step of the journey, and one where I believe only a very small number of businesses are starting to venture today, is into the area of Data Driven P2P Engagement. Again, there are a couple of key elements to think about getting right here.

The first is a proper Data Strategy, which is covered in detail below. This will result in your business being ready to really max out on the benefit of what data can do for it. From the d-Commerce perspective it would be folly to even consider trying to do this before you have worked through Levels 1 to 4.

The other key element is also more strategic in nature, and regards bringing in P2P as a fundamental principle and planning tool for your business to build itself around.

Given the (r)evolution of what it means to be a shopper today, and the consequent seismic shift in the balance of power between the shopper and brand as discussed in Chapter 3, I hope that from the external stakeholder perspective at least you are already considering the merits of a P2P approach. To make the most of this you need to champion this approach internally as well.

There are several key elements to delivering a change initiative successfully in a business: a clear need; alignment; a tangible strategy; upskilling; and in some ways most important of all, demonstration that the change is business additive as it goes along. If you have worked through Levels 1 to 4 of the Maturity Model in sincerity, then expect all of these things to be happening in your business now.

This will then set the scene for the higher-level changes needed to see the job through: those concerning planning, resourcing and strategy in the wider sense. Even better still if you can mirror the d-Commerce Maturity Model in the other key commercial element of your business at the same time (ie in d-Marketing).

A really practical way to make this start coming to life in your business could be to undertake some Purchase Journey Mapping. Where do Sales and Marketing naturally come together? In the P2P of course.

You may be hard pressed to find anyone in your business who could meaningfully counter the razor-sharp logic of that last statement.

What goes around comes around.

There are some perennial discussion topics in d-Commerce, and in particular three have featured prominently throughout my digital journey: Amazon, B2B and Perfect Store.

There will always be a place for a proper and thoroughly executed Perfect Online Store, and I believe that I have covered this in sufficient detail already. To quickly recap: clearly define Look of Success for all d-Commerce subchannels and embed it properly in your business. With regard to Amazon and B2B, it is worth spending a bit more time thinking about these areas again now.

What continues to fascinate about Amazon is that for some businesses it is 1% of their sales and 50% of its conversation. Why is this?

We have all heard the stats: 49% online market share in the US[25]; 15m Prime Subscribers in the UK[26]; 66% product search now starts on Amazon[27] etc so I think it is fairly safe to say that the Pure Play book-sellers of old are worthy of some good coffee machine chitchat at your gaff.

Despite having been pipped to the first ever $1tn company valuation accolade by one of their Silicon Valley BFFs, I think we can probably conclude that it is not a question of *if* Amazon will become the biggest company in the world but *when* (and 2018 incidentally was also the first year that Jeff Bezos was universally recognised as the world's richest person). Amazon has a truly fascinating business model that is worthy of significant study and learning, and I do not have the capacity to do it justice here.

---

[25] Tech Crunch. "Amazon's share of the US e-commerce market is now 49%, or 5% of all retail spend"; https://techcrunch.com/2018/07/13/amazons-share-of-the-us-e-commerce-market-is-now-49-or-5-of-all-retail-spend/ (accessed March 20, 2019).
[26] Mintel. "The Amazon Effect – nine in ten Brits shop on Amazon";
https://www.mintel.com/press-centre/retail-press-centre/the-amazon-effect-nine-in-ten-brits-shop-on-amazon (accessed March 20, 2019).
[27] Feedvisor. "The 2019 Amazon Consumer Behaviour Report";
https://feedvisor.com/resources/amazon-trends/the-2019-amazon-consumer-behavior-report/ (accessed March 20, 2019).

For example, if you even scratch the surface of the fundamental role that Prime plays in their business (both video side and shopping side which are completely intertwined in terms of metrics and objectives), then you start to get a sense of just how clever they are.

The fundamental role of data; the customer obsession; the Test and Learn undertaken on significant scale: hats off to Amazon without a doubt. Amazon will continue to surprise, delight and scare us in equal measure for a few years yet, and it may be that the only credible threats to Jeff's Juggernaut are regulation or some equally clever Chinese folk. Or maybe something that has not been invented yet.

For the relevance to this current d-Commerce discourse, it is worth reflecting on one aspect of the Amazon conversation in particular. The Amazon debate that you hear a lot relates specifically to their position and potential in the UK Grocery Dotcom market, and what brands should do about it.

There are a few perspectives out there, and the polar opposites of expression go something like:

1) 'They are Amazon. Dur. Course they'll be massive in grocery one day. Let's keep disproportionately investing for growth'.

2) 'Amazon? Oh Amazon. They sell groceries now do they? Oo lovely maybe we should do something about it. But aren't my brands already on there? Why is that review bad? And that image? Oh my goodness. Anyhow fix those and that's the Amazon plan sorted. Cheerio'.

I believe that the pragmatic middle ground expression should be:

3) 'Yes, we need an Amazon point of view, but let us think it out carefully. They are only 1% of our business after all, and the Dotcom market in the UK is not the same as the Dotcom market in the US'.

As I have already made the point, do not let the fact that Amazon is Amazon be an Unhealthy Distraction in your business. It is quite possible that there are bigger d-Commerce opportunities for you to think about right now. Tesco is still, and will continue to be for a couple of years at least, the biggest player by some measure. The UK Grocery Dotcom market is the most advanced in the world, so this should be our start point from which to think about exporting learnings if we need to.

Of course, Amazon may purchase one of the UK players at some point. When and if this happens there will be plenty to do on terms and business alignment to incline you to not be too amenable to stretching commercial demands today in my view.

If 50% of your business chitchat was around unlocking d-Commerce more holistically, then you would bring significantly more benefit to your top and bottom lines over the time frames that really matter in CPG: the short and medium terms. I am not saying you do not need an Amazon strategy or point of view, of course you do. They could (and probably will) surprise us at some point. All I am suggesting is that some proportionality may be helpful *today,* especially if you are just stepping out on your d-Commerce journey.

The reason Amazon is 50% of your business's conversation is quite possibly because it deserves to be. There has quite simply never been such a disruptive force in (literally) the world of retail. But do not let that be an Unhealthy Distraction from the 1% (or maybe that should be the other 99%?) in the equation too.

After all, the UK CPG d-Commerce market is ripe with the fruit of opportunity. One fruit which is very much a Healthy Distraction and may be ready to pick, right now, is the B2B subchannel.

The wholesale cash and carry sector (B2B) is a £11.5bn sales channel[28] where 50% of your sales could already be occurring online. Yes, you did read that correctly.

Imagine for a moment if 50% of your sales through Tesco were occurring

---

[28] IGD. "UK grocery & foodservice wholesaling 2017"; https://www.igd.com/Portals/0/Downloads/Events/UKGroceryFoodserviceWholesaling20 17.pdf (accessed March 20, 2019).

online. I am sure that would have quite a profound effect in your business with regard to its speed of d-Commerce opportunity recognition and adoption.

The B2B sector is traditionally one that is considered to be a bit of a murky backwater in our industry, and not necessarily the first port of call if you are looking for a land of opportunity; especially a digital one. In some ways B2B is a backwater, but when it comes to share of business online, Tesco et al are just *so* last century.

Many of the main B2B players are already touting a total share of business sold online of up to about a third[29]. In specific categories this is much higher: 50% or more. The reason for this, in simple terms, is because B2B's Primary Shoppers (ie the small store owners) have woken up apace to the benefits of ordering their stock online rather than going into depot and selecting it physically.

Ordering online for the small store owner ticks many of the Online Channel Triggers that we discussed above: it can be done at any time via a range of handy devices and saves a trip to the depot. If the B2B retailer throws in free delivery, then even better. And herein lies a very real business opportunity.

If you spend a bit of time on a B2B website, you will soon appreciate that the SX can be in a backwater compared to the Dotcoms. Granted some sites are better than others, but overall there is much that can be done to tap into Triggers and Barriers thinking that will result in tangible cash benefit fairly readily.

The SX in B2B does need to be different in some ways from Dotcom. The need to provide wider information (eg opening hours, depot info, margin calculators) must be thought through and incorporated as appropriate into your Perfect B2B Store. However, everything that you do for Fix the Basics in the Dotcoms needs to be repeated for the B2B sites, with due consideration to the dual needs of both the Primary (small store owner) and the Secondary (small store customer) Shopper.

---

[29] Eg Booker, Bestway and Parfetts.

One throwback that you may come across is that it is difficult to get to grips with the B2B channel because of the available data. Whilst it is true that the big data houses fuelling your business reporting in the other channels do not have anywhere near as robust a read here as they do for Big Box retail, do not for a minute assume that there is a business inhibiting paucity of data in B2B.

There is data available, some of it is just a bit different and to be found in slightly different places. Whilst it may not yet be dropped into your business with the same regularity as the weekly or monthly big data house stuff, there is definitely enough data available to work through the first few levels of the d-Commerce Maturity Model, for example.

And whilst you are at it, howsabout getting dirty with a nice B2B dashboard to raise the opportunity profile in your business too?

The final point to make in this 'what goes around comes around' inspired trip down d-Commerce memory lane, is that we were recently asked to help build a B2B Channel Strategy. Not only did this involve evaluating the SX, looking at the Size of the Prize, building the trade and internal engagement story, but we were also asked to create a strategic framework too.

The framework that we put forward? The exact same iteration of The 4 Ps that was shared with the world first time around. If you wait long enough then things always come back into fashion at some point.

Data in focus #5: Don't start with the tech.

Do not waste any of your hard-earned business cash on technology solutions without first working through an overall Data Strategy. If you do go down the tech route first, then there is a very realistic chance that you will be wasting money. Do not buy a Ferrari if your business does not need one, there is no fuel to put in the tank, and no one knows how to drive it safely anyhow.

You can start off with a Data Strategy purely focused on generating some of the Eureka moments talked about in Chapter 4. If your business is ready to move towards a different data destination than this, then it could well be worth building a Data Strategy around four specific areas:

1) Collect. Aside from business reporting requirements, what data does your business need to collect to better understand its shoppers and consumers? What options are there out there? What are the pros and cons of each?

   These are all crucial questions to spend a bit of time working through, and if you are not sure, do not overcommit and Test and Learn instead. You may not even need to invest a significant amount of money to get started with collection at all: there are plenty of online gizmos available which are easy to set up and run.

   As you go further down the collection route, there are of course much more sophisticated options available to you. Again, always start off with a clear view on the question/s you are trying to answer, or a hypothesis to test if you prefer. You will always get more business additive insight from your data, either from a simple dataset or more complex aggregated anonymised ones, if you start with a sensible problem statement.

2) Governance. Crucial to go hand in hand with your collection approach is a robust view on governance. If you are not sure here then this would be a good place to ask for expert help.

   Proper management of data is, for good reason, receiving an increasing amount of attention. This is true of the law (GDPR applies to all businesses of a certain size and can result in a fine of 4% of global turnover for breaches), as well as for the softer currency of business reputation.

   Facebook, for example, has received a lot of bad press in the last year or two as a result of concerns around how it is managing its users' data. Each time this happens their share price takes a significant hit. Having the right governance policies in place is very important.

Within governance I would also include things like scorecards and reporting. Is your data telling the most useful story for its recipients? Is your data getting the points across that you want it to and in the most impactful way? My own personal data journey began with Retail Link when I was a Category Analyst at Kraft Foods, and it was an incredibly useful Box 2 exercise to spend a bit of time understanding exactly what the customer did, and did not, need to receive every Monday morning.

3) Execute. Next, think about what you actually want your data to do. Who do you want to target with it? How are you going to execute a business strategy through it? This is especially important when you move on to more sophisticated practices like P2P Engagement.

   Manipulation of different datasets offers a whole range of mass or targeted execution options for your data. Again, maybe start small with a Test and Learn before diving in with a whole new automated plan and solution.

   This is also a good place to get to grips with ideas like audience mapping, combining different datasets, lookalike modelling etc. Although such practices may at first appear quite esoteric, they really are not that complicated when you approach them in the right way with a willingness to learn.

4) Measurement. This is the final key pillar of any successful Data Strategy, and potentially the most simplistic and complicated at the same time. You need to develop a clear view of whether your data is telling you if something is working or not which is a simple concept; there can unfortunately be a whole host of Unhealthy Distractions that can get in the way of straightforward interpretation.

   You may never get a full answer which I think is absolutely fine. If you can get 80% of an answer (sometimes any answer will do!) with 20% of the puzzle complete then let Pareto rule: Test, Learn, Modify,

Test, Learn, Move on.

Of course, as you travel down the d-Commerce path, then over time your business will likely require more sophisticated measurement techniques, and some businesses are firmly in this place today. For the majority (the 80% again I would argue), starting out with some basic data-led d-Commerce measurement would be progress along the Space- Time continuum for sure.

When you have got the bones of a Data Strategy built around these four areas, this might be a good time to think about a more structured Test and Learn programme for all the different enablers of data driven success in your business.

Again, this need not be a scary thing to do. If we assume that all businesses are somewhere on a Basic, Intermediate, and Advanced axis with regard to their overall data maturity, then it is absolutely possible to develop a congruent approach to move towards the light and unlock the power of data in your business.

This overall approach can work on a number of levels. For example, if we have a desire to improve the data driven SX, then we can start breaking down what this means across our four Data Strategy pillars. If we just need to start off by articulating what on earth we are talking about, then this approach will work too.

If you lay all this out clearly at a Basic, Intermediate and Advanced level, then this would provide a very structured data framework to start working through. By also overlaying some case studies, this will further reassure your business that you will ultimately deliver commercial benefit by following the data path. This could also provide a 'safe' way to start thinking about reconciling what is the dark side of data for some: uncertainty around data tech.

Remember, start off with a clearly crafted problem statement and a layered and embedded understanding of success. Follow this path towards the light and you really do have nothing to fear. Remember that fear is the path to the dark side (uncertainty around data tech). Fear leads to Anger. Anger leads to hate. Hate leads to suffering.

Before we know it we may even start to feel like Level 1 data Jedis (or like slightly less confused Padawans at least).

Hopefully now your own data love is thinking about creeping in too, and the data fog starting to clear. If it is not, then maybe go back to Page 1 and start again.

d-Commerce Decoded in byte sized chunks.

- Have an operational d-Commerce plan that links together the high-level strategy and its implementation on the ground.
- When the basics are fixed, have a clear idea of what to do next.
- Work at the level of d-Commerce sophistication that is right for your business then move on.
- Always start with the SX. Bring this into your d-Commerce Channel Strategy.
- Deliver Omnichannel Shopper Marketing solutions.
- Only think more widely about Capability Development at the right time.
- Have answers ready to the perennial d-Commerce questions.
- Lay out what to do with data collection, governance, execution and measurement first.
- Start with a problem statement, not a tech solution.

CHAPTER 6. BILL GATES WAS WRONG

Quote; me happy.

ABSOLUTELY LOVE a good quote, and one of my all-time besties is from everyone's favourite nerd, the genre defining tech billionaire Bill Gates.

In his 1996 book, *The Road Ahead*, Mr Gates proudly postulates that "we always overestimate the change that will occur in the next two years and underestimate the change that will occur in the next ten"[30].

Well I am sorry Bill, but based on the most recent two years in every single person's life, in every single household, in every single country around the world you have been proved wrong. Very wrong.

In all fairness to Mr Microsoft, I do not believe that anybody could have got close to overestimating the change that was coming in those pre-pandemic halcyon days of early 2020. The COVID 19 pandemic has had, and is still having, an unprecedented level of impact in pretty much every aspect of all our lives.

---

[30] Bill Gates, *The Road Ahead*, (Viking Penguin, US, 1996).

Being in no position of authority to give many of these innumerable aspects anything other than subjective consideration, the pandemic's relevance to the current tome shall be considered on a single plane only: the impact on online shopping. And in the couple of years that have elapsed since I completed Chapter 5, that impact has been massive.

According to Kantar, at the end of 2019 in the UK, just under 8% of CPG transactions were made online[31]. Two years later in December 2021 that figure was 12.2%, after peaking at 15.4% in February that year[32]; and that is quite a shift.

Yes, it is fair to say that the pandemic merely turned up the heat on a change in shopping behaviour that had been slowly bubbling away for a few years; yes, it is fair to say that – as the data shows – the change has cooled slightly in the last few months; and yes, it is fair to say that the shift towards more online shopping will occur into the future.

So now, more than ever, is the time to take action! (And in all fairness to Bill Gates, the next sentence in his book after the one quoted above is "Don't let yourself be lulled into inaction"[33]; so maybe everything he says is not complete nonsense after all).

And taking action many brands are. But are they taking the right action? There has definitely been a fairly widespread upweight in e-Commerce headcount in lots of businesses, and one or two are even talking about having more money to invest; so the 'throwing resources at it' approach is definitely on the road ahead for many at the start of 2022.

But how well have the foundations of that road been laid? How well are the signposts anchored and illuminated along the way? And how many of us really know where that road is even going? Time for another quote:

---

[31] Kantar, *10 thoughts on COVID-19 and its impact on purchase and consumption behaviour*, 30th June 2020.
[32] BBC News, "Kantar: Shoppers return to supermarkets for festive feasts"; https://www.bbc.com/news/business-59880116 (accessed 8th February, 2022).
[33] Gates, *The Road Ahead*.

"There is nothing either good or bad, but thinking makes it so"[34].

Or in other words, do not just assume that just because everyone is talking about something, that they are talking about the right thing. I believe that we always need to be careful not to drink the e-Commerce Kool Aid, avoiding the temptation to jump into a thing based on perception alone.

Now clearly e-Commerce, per se, is a very big thing indeed; but under the e-Commerce umbrella can shelter many an Unhealthy Distraction as explained way back in Chapter 1.

An Unhealthy Distraction that has become apparent in the last couple of years:

1) Voice Commerce.

And what could possibly be the next one:

2) Quick Commerce (or Rapid Grocery Delivery or On Demand Groceries or etc).

I feel that I need to explain my thinking here. With regard to Voice Commerce, I stated at its moment of immaculate materialisation that caution may be a virtue, and let us be honest, Voice has not come to dominate (or even slightly pester) commerce or search since then.

Brands the world over went on a Voice enabled spending spree and got nowhere; a more prudent Test and Learn approach would have made sense (and a profile view from a 'Global Head of Voice Commerce' at a major CPG multinational when I blogged about the fact that Voice became a whisper made me smile, as I appreciated that at least one brand had maybe got a bit carried away).

Which moves us on to point 2.

---

[34] William Shakespeare, *Hamlet,* (Nicholas Ling and John Trundell, UK, 1603).

At the time of writing, Quick Commerce is the plat du jour in many CPG businesses. Playbooks are being written, jobs are being created, and the LinkedIn news feed quite literally overflows with articles on eye watering investments, mega mergers and crazy stats on a daily basis (including the questionable claim that the 123% rise in grocery delivery app spend in the last five months of 2021 correlated with a 22% drop in spend in convenience stores in the same period[35]; but then again, 39% of statistics are made up).

Although sales volumes from some players are starting to look interesting, I think for the long-term perspective that at best the jury should be out on Quick Commerce. Sensible brands are going down the Test and Learn route; others I believe really have drunk the Kool Aid and gone all in, and quite frankly quite a few VCs are off their heads.

The issue with Quick Commerce is the (cost to serve) operating model. I just do not believe that when the slowing of online shopping growth meets the rising cost of goods in the post pandemic world, that enough shoppers (or brands) will be prepared to pick up the tab needed replenish the VC bank accounts. And while that is clearly a shame on many levels, I think brands need to be careful that they do not divert too many valuable resources into Quick Commerce at this time.

In markets like the UK, where there already exists a perfectly adequate grocery delivery service, I believe the obsession with delivery speed is an Unhealthy Distraction. A watching brief and some category appropriate Testing and Learning is the best way to proceed for now.

So where do I think the Healthy Distractions are today? I am still backing B2B and by extension Marketplaces as worthy of serious investigation right now. B2B e-Commerce is still the sleeping giant of online, and is due a noisy wake up.

Quick B2B tasting menu: for starters do some opportunity sizing and define a strategy covering three main areas: core wholesale; direct

---

[35]https://internetretailing.net/mobile-theme/mobile-theme/the-rise-of-rapid-delivery-apps-eats-into-grocery-market-share-24238 (accessed February 16, 2022).

sales; Marketplaces (eg Amazon Business; eBay; Alibaba.com). For main course do some Fix the Basics type work at the B2B Digital Shelf. And then for dessert get stuck in to some sweet tasting Revenue Growth Management (RGM) and the nuances of maximising the impact of your profile / account wherever you are selling. And if you need a napkin and a knife and fork to help your business digest it all, then please just ask.

Clearly no-one can predict the future and even the most sensible thinkers can get completely wrong footed by unexpected global events. However, do not let this put you off!

Despite all the Unhealthy and Healthy Distractions, the reality is that winning e-Commerce is actually a sum of marginal gains. To win, it is advisable to strike the right balance between maximising your opportunity with the big safe bets like Dotcom Grocery, and appropriately checking out some interesting new stuff like B2B. Do this, and chances are that you will not go far wrong.

Do the right things and the right things will happen. Take some balanced risks and if all else fails just put your best foot forwards and tell yourself that "this time next year Rodney we'll be millionaires"[36].

But how do you know what the right things to do are? Time for some good practical advice about giving yourself the best chance of making that deeply profound aphorism come true.

Get some maturity with PACE.

As explained in Chapter 5, an area where businesses genuinely appreciate and often need guidance is with a maturity roadmap: where to start their e-Commerce journey and how to become advanced practitioners.

When Daedal started we helped brands meet that need via our Digital

---

[36] Del Boy.

Commerce Maturity Model as can be seen on page 83 above. But things have got *way* more interesting since then: now it is all about PACE.

Figure 9: PACE Maturity Framework.

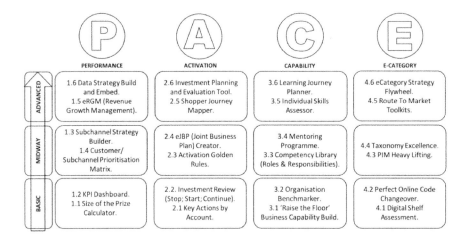

The basic premise of PACE is twofold:

1) In order to enable sustainable d-Commerce commercial growth, brands need to focus on four areas: Performance; Activation; Capability; E-Category.
2) Within each area brands need to move from a Basic to an Advanced level of practice.

To help brands on this journey we have defined a clear set of toolkits and approaches that are laid out in the model above. In reality brands may well already be doing some or many of these things; we have so far only come across one who has confidently told us that all bases are covered and no PACE is required.

To quickly walk through the various stages of maturity across the four PACE areas:

With regard to Performance, we believe you should always start by defining the unrestrained opportunity for d-Commerce in your business. Our way of approaching this is laid out above on page 69, and has not changed significantly over the last couple of years, although clearly now there is often more data to plug into the ten step process. Next, work through KPIs and dashboarding (either manual or automated), and all your Performance Basics are covered.

For Midway Performance, we recommend conducting a proper prioritisation exercise across your customer and subchannel base, rather than either following a 's/he who shouts loudest' or plat du jour approach to resource allocation.

A way that we have done this for clients successfully is via the Will, Skill and Importance matrix laid out below. In the spirit of kaizen advocated throughout this book, this matrix is a positive evolution of the approach laid out above on page 62.

Rather than just considering 'effort' and 'reward', we now recommend looking at three different metrics to assess where to prioritise your efforts: Will is all about how willing the customer (or subchannel) is to work with you; Skill is how able they are; Importance is the future importance (revenue potential) of that customer or subchannel to your business.

Figure 10: Will, Skill and Importance Prioritisation Matrix.

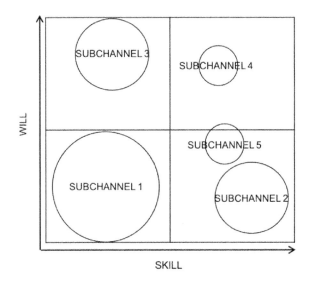

Will and Skill are plotted on the relevant axes, and Importance is included relative to circle size (ie the bigger the circle, the more important).

By prioritising this way you can make some sensible calls around how to invest on a subchannel by subchannel, or customer by customer, basis. Additionally, depending on in which quadrant the subchannel or customer sits, you can also deploy a different type of eJBP or engagement strategy.

This is also a great feed into the remaining elements of reaching Advanced Performance Maturity: the right Subchannel Strategies, what to do about Products, Pricing and Promotions and ultimately how to get the most from your data.

For Activation, start by really getting into the weeds of what is happening in your business on an account by account basis: what is your qualitative and quantitative account specific data telling you? (ie being really clear on the 'why' behind the numbers). Then you can develop specific actions to fix any problems over a thirty day, three month and twelve month timescale (also known as the 'how' and the 'what'; Simon Sinek Golden Circle[37] refresher endeth here).

Then think more about investment: looking at the last twenty-four months of d-Commerce spending in your business, what should you Start doing, what should you Stop doing and what should you Continue doing? Many businesses still lack this basic understanding of how to spend their d-Commerce bitcoin in the most efficient way possible.

To achieve Midway Activation Maturity, take these learnings up a notch and ensure that your eJBPs are tailored depending on level of customer sophistication (link back to Will, Skill and Importance). And it goes without saying that you need to ensure that all your Activation is hitting the gold standard by now too.

---

[37] Sinek, *Start With Why: How Great Leaders Inspire Everyone To Take Action*.

Finally, fine tune your Activation Strategy. Do this in two principle ways:

1) Pile all the insight you can into building a robust Omnichannel Shopper Journey Map, so you can really understand your opportunities and blind spots from the shoppers' point of view.

2) Deliver laser focused campaigns. We think the best way to do this is to deploy a shiny Investment Planning and Evaluation gizmo into all the relevant parts of your business.

So that is Performance and Activation sorted. The final two parts of this chapter are dedicated to talking through Capability and E-Category as quite frankly there is an awful lot to say here. We will look at E-Category first.

Time to up your game: Amazon have got nothing on this.

The Digital Shelf will always be a crucial foundation of your d-Commerce efforts. There is much guidance and many third-party solutions than can help here, although it is interesting to note that post the automated shelf scraping tool gold rush, some brands are starting to question the value of these solutions in their businesses.

This is for a couple of reasons. As with all automated tools there can be a challenge on breadth and depth of usage in the business, and cost is a consideration too. Some brands have also realised that they can actually do a fairly good job themselves by deployment of a methodology like SCANR, where Search, Content, Availability, Navigation and Reviews and manually appraised from the Shopper Experience (SX) perspective. Whatever your chosen approach is, E-Category Basics must start here.

The next couple of steps on the E-Category Maturity journey are possibly not the most shiny ones your business will ever take, but in terms of impact on revenue they can be significant (good or bad!).

Online Code Changeovers need careful and proper management. Due to the way retailer site algorithms work, there is a real risk of negatively affecting fundamental sales drivers like availability, search performance or favourites inclusion if the changeover is not managed properly. This can all cost a lot of money to put right, and may even damage the brand perception that the relaunch or shrinkflation inspired code changeover sought to positively boost. You need to work very carefully with your wider business and retail partners over an extended time period to minimise this risk.

To move to Midway E-Category Maturity, think about your PIM (Product Information Management – or in plain English, the way that your brand copy appears on retailer websites).

If your business still has not sorted its online product images then quite frankly you should feel ashamed; however, do not chastise yourself quite so much when it comes to the accompanying copy as this is actually an area of low hanging fruit for many brands.

Your copy needs to work on a number of levels, although primarily to stack the retailer algorithm odds in your favour and also to keep your shoppers happy. (Note that to keep your marketer colleagues happy is actually priority three here – sorry brand folk).

Broadly speaking you will get the most from your PIM by ensuring that the product forms being sent to Brandbank contain copy that is search optimised, retailer site compliant and enabled, and full of language shoppers will find useful and understand. And make sure that you sit on / incentivise your retailer partners to pull the new information through if it has been updated, as that is quite important too.

Another opportunity you have to work more closely with your retail partners is on taxonomy (the hierarchy of product classifications in the department or category pages on the retailer site – a bit like the online equivalent of instore shelf layout).

Although opportunities to work with retailers on the taxonomy in your category may not come around often, it is still important to understand and maximise the ease of shop potential of this E-Category stalwart. (And this can be a good area to demonstrate expertise in some of the emerging d-Commerce subchannels too).

You can think about taxonomy optimisation in a number of ways: what to do if you are data rich or data lite; how you translate a Shopper Decision Hierarchy (SDH) to a retailer website; what are all the different parts of the site where your brands have fair cause to appear.

What you do not need to do to bring some good old Pareto 80:20 benefits to your business, is invest in a potentially expensive quantitative or qualitative study.

A few taxonomy golden rules to consider to get started:

1) Minimise the number of clicks (through a taxonomy) required to find an actual product. The ideal number is three.
2) Strip out duplication (ie so products sit in one part of the hierarchy only) to avoid potential confusion.
3) Use shopper language, and where you can follow the SDH. If you do not have an online SDH then an offline one is an absolutely fine place to start.
4) Consider some final filters at the lowest level of the hierarchy to help shoppers choose (eg sugar or no sugar).
5) And if you really are just starting out, then spend some time clicking through the taxonomy as it is today so you get a basic understanding of how it works.

The Advanced E-Category practices concern Route To Market toolkits (also sometimes called subchannel toolkits), and the real jewel in the crown: the e-Category Flywheel. We will consider Route To Market toolkits first of all.

Thanks to the good old internet, brands have many more Routes To Market than they did a few years ago. Yes they can still use those Bricks and Mortar shop things, but now you can also use a few others as well: Quick Commerce; B2B; D2C; Marketplaces all now at your virtual fingertips. It is important to build all of these toolkits from the category perspective, as this will give the most rounded guidance on what to do.

Quick Route To Market (RTM) toolkit inclusion checklist. Make sure you shiny PDF or PowerPoint covers four main areas:

1) An introduction to the RTM, who the main players are, its size and growth, and how it fits into your business's overall strategy.
2) What your ambition is for the RTM (eg Size of the Prize or distribution gains).
3) A 'how to win' action plan including both basics such as The Digital Shelf and more advanced elements such as Revenue Growth Management or a Data Strategy.
4) Any case studies of other brands' efforts.

Include all those things properly and embed the toolkit into your business (with adequate resources included), and your colleagues will be inspired to unlock and deliver new brand sales.

And talking of inspiration, and taking a big chunk of it from the virtuous growth cycle that sits at the heart of Amazon's business, The Amazon Flywheel, the final part of this Chapter covers something very shiny indeed: the e-Category Flywheel.

At the time of writing, Amazon are not quite able to 'get' the merits of deploying classic CPG Category Vision or Category Strategy online, so they really do not have anything on this. They would however definitely get the idea of putting a cyclical and virtuous sales growth framework at the heart of a business.

Unlike Amazon, now your business can have double bubble, both getting such Category Strategy merits, and also setting a virtuous growth cycle at the centre of its sales driving efforts. It can do this by deploying the e-Category Flywheel. This will also then enable you to win the next major CPG battleground of Online Category Vision, or e-Cat Strat if you prefer.

The e-Category Flywheel is basically a roadmap that your business can follow to simultaneously translate your existing Category Vision to online, whilst also delivering incremental growth to both your and your customers' businesses.

Never forget that there are only three ways to deliver incremental sales online: steal from your competitors (brand happy, retailer indifferent unless there is a margin mix benefit); steal from instore (no-one happy apart from the narrow minded e-Commerce P&L owner); grow the category (brand happy, retailer happy). I think you should focus on option 3.

In virtually all product categories there exists today the opportunity for first mover advantage in e-Cat Strat, and an opportunity to take something new and of real value to your retail partners.

Figure 11: The e-Category Flywheel.

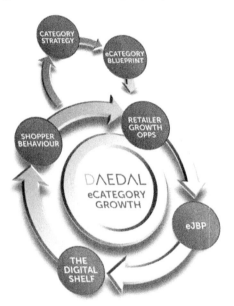

To deploy the Flywheel into your business, start off with your existing Cat Strat and from this build out an e-Category Blueprint, for example defining which of your Category Drivers are particularly relevant for online.

Then clearly articulate these in terms of retailer growth opportunities, ensuring your engagement and thinking is as retailer and shopper focused as possible. Next, construct an eJBP which is conducive to supporting category activation before deploying the right tactics at The Digital Shelf, thereby influencing shopper behaviour.

Finally, feed the relevant output of this back into your overall Category Strategy and go around again.

I have always believed passionately in a 'Category First' approach to any kind of selling, as this delivers win:win:wins for brand, retailer and shopper. Deploy the e-Category Flywheel into your business and your key retail partners, and you really are at the pinnacle of E-Category Maturity.

And my other great passion is building capability.

Data in Focus #6: The right way to address Digital Capability.

Building sustainable Digital Commerce capability, with a clear link to sustainable commercial growth, is the holy grail of Digital Commerce-dom, and has been a constant bedfellow of my own Digital Commerce journey of the last ten plus years.

I covered on page 38 above the wrong way to address Digital Capability; in summary: do not assume anything or reach for a boiler plate training package when someone in your business thinks capability building is needed.

There were also some thoughts on some more positive steps to take; in summary: find out what your business really needs and do the job properly, deploying some key principles like 70:20:10 and Learning Journeys.

All of these summary points are still valid.

What we have now though is the crème de la crème of Digital Commerce capability building, and it all starts with our old friend data.

At the end of 2021, Daedal launched a new capability hub to the market which after literally minutes of deliberation we decided to call d-BUG, standing for Benchmark; Unlock; Grow.

In the much longer process of development, we deployed many of the positive ways of working advocated in this book. These included fairly extensive testing and learning with some great brand partners, input from many very helpful SMEs, and constant agile working in the development process. And quite a lot of head scratching and hard work too.

The basic premise of d-BUG is a system of three interconnected modules, as explained by the diagram below.

Figure 12: d-BUG Hub Architecture.

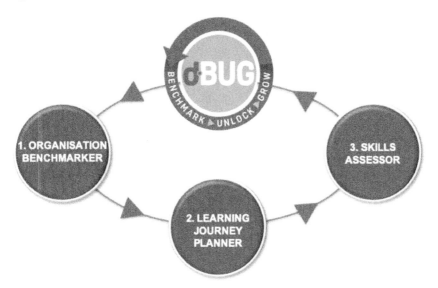

The place to start is with Organisation Benchmarker, and this enables all that follows to be built with the e-Commerce alchemist's potion of dreams: data. Additionally, there are a number of key principles which underpin the overall approach.

The first principle of the right way to address Digital Commerce capability is to look first at the organisation. There is no point commissioning e-Commerce training for your employees unless you are very clear on exactly what they need training on, otherwise you will just waste a load of money frankly.

Within Organisational Benchmarker sits a framework of eight Organisational Competencies each split into three elements, so twenty-four elements in total. The Organisational Competencies are Leadership Focus; Providing Clarity; Integrated Planning; Available Resources; Setting Up To Win; Winning With Retailers; e-Category Development; Data and Insight. Taken together these competencies and elements cover all the requisite areas successful e-Commerce businesses have in common, and so by adopting them in your business, you can become successful at e-Commerce too.

Then, through a combination of self and facilitated assessment, organisations can understand *exactly* where their Digital Commerce strengths and opportunities lie against these competencies, by comparing their business to a CPG benchmark. This gives a data driven understanding of exactly where to focus, and also nicely tees up Module 2: Learning Journey Planner.

Learning Journey Planner covers all that is good in developing effective learning solutions, part of which is enabling you to make the most of your existing internal resource so you only bring in (pay for) external expertise where there is a genuine need. Layer over effective 70:20:10 blended capability plans and you are away.

Working in tandem, Organisation Benchmarker and Learning Journey Planner set you up with exactly the capability solutions that your business requires to plug its unique gaps.

Now if only there was a third part of a triumvirate that demonstrated the effectiveness of those learning plans over time. As luck would have it Module 3, Skills Assessor, contributes exactly that.

The final key principle of d-BUG is that businesses should be able to demonstrate the effectiveness of their Learning and Development programme (and return on its budget). This growth principle sits at the heart of Module 3.

One way to demonstrate the effectiveness of any learning solution is to help every individual in the business to understand exactly where they are today, and how they improve over time. d-BUG does exactly that by defining what Digital Commerce competency profile is required for each individual's particular combination of function and seniority, and then shows the individual where their strengths and opportunities are versus that target profile and how they change (improve!) over time. The Module can also serve as a very useful framework for defining the right e-Commerce Roles and Responsibilities that your business may need.

By assessing individuals in this way we create a data-driven record, and progress can be tangibly demonstrated against a target over time.

That is right, everyone in your business needs to develop a level of Digital Commerce capability, and everyone in your business can be assessed on what progress they are making too.

And on that bombshell...

Bill Gates Was Wrong in byte sized chunks.

- d-Commerce is becoming more important in the CPG industry, and that importance has increased significantly in the last couple of years.
- Approach Quick Commerce with a test and learn mindset, and back B2B as the next big subchannel bet.
- Break your d-Commerce approach into four principle areas: Performance; Activation; Capability; E-Category. Work to achieve an advanced level of maturity in each area over time.
- Prioritise your d-Commerce resources by subchannel and / or customer, and tailor your approach based on priority level.
- Winning the E-Category is about much more than delivering at The Digital Shelf. Understand if there is an opportunity to develop a Category Strategy (or Category Vision) that is tailored for online.
- Develop the most effective capability plan for your business by starting with a comprehensive understanding of your strengths and opportunities at the organisational level.
- Make the most of your existing internal capability resource before paying for external expertise.

- Make sure you can demonstrate return for your Learning and Development investment. One way to do this is by defining and tracking progress against individual target competency profiles over time.

CONCLUSION. TEN GIGA-BYTES

I N OUR SNACKABLE content obsessed digital world, it seems only appropriate to conclude my monologue with a summary of the main points raised above. What are the key things you should start doing, right now, if you want to bring more of the d-Commerce Dollar into your business bank account? My ten giga-bytes would be:

1) Understand how your shoppers experience your brands across all d-Commerce subchannels. Fix the basic fruit that hangs so low it is virtually touching the ground.

2) Calculate the Size of the Prize at subchannel and Shopper Measure level then prioritise resources.

3) Split your d-Commerce plans into the four constituent parts of Performance, Activation, Capability and E-Category. Then work to improve business maturity in each of these areas over time.

4) Embolden change agents to champion d-Commerce in your business. Make them fully accountable and let them deliver. Do not ever forget the Marzipan Layer.

5) Test and Learn a lot, especially when something really new and interesting comes along.

6) Let Shopper Marketing shine and do lots of Shiny Things. Accept that you might have to do some non-Shiny Things too to win.

7) Think omnichannel in everything you do. Harmonise internally and externally via a P2P approach.

8) Build a Data Strategy before a tech stack. Beware of Unhealthy Distractions and improve focus on ROI.

9) If you want something really new and interesting to take to your retail partners, create an e-Cat Strat.

10) Build capability in the right way. The right way is to start by understanding the picture at the organisational level and end by demonstrating growth at the individual level.

AFTERWORD TO THE SECOND EDITION

I FORMALLY LAUNCHED Daedal with the tagline 'd-Commerce Decoded' in 2018. The business is a CPG consultancy with a clear mission: to be our clients' partner of choice for sustainable Digital Commerce commercial and capability growth.

Daedal is built around three distinct solutions which, I believe, are exactly what CPG manufacturers need to help them sell more and win the omnichannel shopper. I would heartily encourage you to visit www.daedal.uk or scan the QR code on the back cover to find out more. In brief, the three solutions are the PACE Maturity Framework, the e-Category Flywheel and the d-BUG Capability Hub.

These solutions have evolved and emerged as a result of working with a wide range of businesses and categories during my own d-Commerce journey over the last ten years and counting. The essence, rationale, and direct experience of delivering these solutions are peppered throughout this book.

There may be some questions that Daedal cannot immediately answer, and the benefit we could bring to some businesses will be more or less marked than in others. However, we are yet to engage a business where something that we think or have done has not sparked a pilot light of interest at least!

As has been the case since I first nervously ambled towards the d-Commerce precipice at UB, I have benefitted significantly from other people's wisdom along the way. There are a number of mentors and peers who have been incredibly helpful at various times, some with more awareness of this than others, and I thank you all. These people are named specifically in the Words of Thanks on the final page.

In this vein, it is noteworthy that the final part of the Daedal puzzle itself actually crystallised on the back of an impromptu coaching session with a former colleague. After a gap of over ten years, I reconnected with a chap from Kraft who had recently left the helm of an evolution of that very same company in the UK. He was instrumental in helping me to work out what to do at a critical juncture in my career, and for that I am particularly thankful.

In the true Test and Learn d-Commerce spirit advocated throughout this book, I fully intend to never stop learning, and never stop sharing the nuggets that have helped me. I encourage you to do the same!

We would of course welcome the opportunity to discuss any of the ideas expressed in this book with you in person, and in true omnichannel spirit both virtual and physical meetings are possible. If this is something that you would like to do then just drop me a line: marc@daedal.uk.

Thanks for taking the time to read my little book. Now go forth and Digitally Commerce!

Marc

WORDS OF THANKS

For helping me along the way whether you knew it or not: Keith Higgins, Paul Barry-Walsh, Jamie Holland, Jon Eggleton, Paul Graham, James Coupland, Rose Price, Simon Miles, Alessandro Arosio, Tom Benton, Michael Aidan, Fox, Tim Westwell, Sebastian Pole, Tim Heydon, David Martin, Mark Davies, Mike Taylor, Nick Broomfield, Stefan Minchev, David Bone, Sean Teehan, Ant Duffin, Andrew Cowen, Andy Tosney.

For helping me Test and Learn the various versions of the book you have just read: Paul Waterson, David Eldridge, Hamish Paton, Stu Heffernan, Jan Boyle, Neil Woodcock, Viv Craske, Jamie Warburton, Julie Warburton.

Printed in Great Britain
by Amazon

80176219R00078